USBORNE
FACTS & FUN
ABOUT
ANIMALS AND SCIENCE

USBORNE
FACTS & FUN
ABOUT
ANIMALS AND SCIENCE

SCHOLASTIC INC.
New York Toronto London Auckland Sydney

ISBN 0-590-62144-0

12 11 10 9 8 7 6 5 4   8 9/9 0/0

Printed in the U.S.A.   08

First Scholastic printing, September 1995

Contents

USBORNE
FACTS & FUN
ABOUT
ANIMALS AND SCIENCE

Part One

USBORNE FACTS & FUN ABOUT ANIMALS

Paul Dowswell

Edited by Judy Tatchell

Designed by Ruth Russell

Illustrated by Ian Jackson and Rachel Lockwood

Additional illustrations by Chris Lyon and John Shackell

Consultant: Gillian Standring

Contents

About Part One

There are over two million different kinds of animal in the world. Even baking deserts, the frozen poles, and the deepest oceans have their own unique inhabitants. Part One of the book looks at how animals behave, and how they cope with the different environments in which they live.

How to do the quizzes

Throughout the book, there are quiz questions to answer as you go along, printed in italic type, *like this*. Some of the questions rely on your general knowledge, others have clues elsewhere on the page. Keep a note of your answers and check them against the answers on page 28-31.

The Animal Megaquiz

On pages 26-27 is the Animal Megaquiz – a set of ten quick quizzes to test you on what you have read in Part One. You can check your answers on page 32.

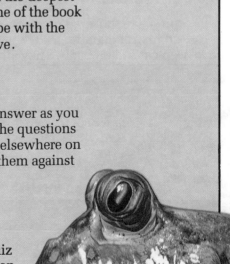

The animal world

There are an extraordinary number of different sizes, shapes and colors in the animal world. These two pages look at the main types of animals and how they fit into their environment.

Scientists have divided the animal world into various groups. Animals in the same group, or class, have similar features, and behave in similar ways. A particular kind of animal, such as a lion or an ostrich, is known as a species. Some of the main groups are shown here.

The animal groups shown in the circles are:

Mammals	Molluscs
Birds	Insects
Crustaceans	Reptiles
Amphibians	Fish

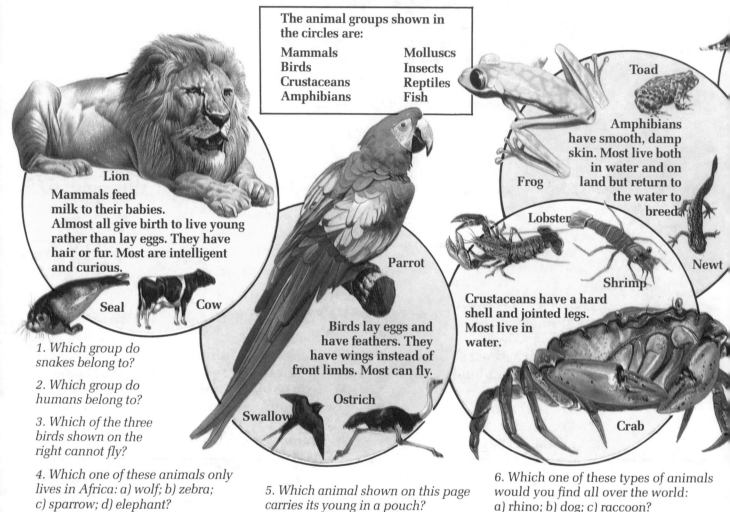

Lion
Mammals feed milk to their babies. Almost all give birth to live young rather than lay eggs. They have hair or fur. Most are intelligent and curious.

Seal

Cow

Parrot

Birds lay eggs and have feathers. They have wings instead of front limbs. Most can fly.

Ostrich

Swallow

Toad

Amphibians have smooth, damp skin. Most live both in water and on land but return to the water to breed.

Frog

Newt

Lobster

Shrimp

Crustaceans have a hard shell and jointed legs. Most live in water.

Crab

1. Which group do snakes belong to?

2. Which group do humans belong to?

3. Which of the three birds shown on the right cannot fly?

4. Which one of these animals only lives in Africa: a) wolf; b) zebra; c) sparrow; d) elephant?

5. Which animal shown on this page carries its young in a pouch?

6. Which one of these types of animals would you find all over the world: a) rhino; b) dog; c) raccoon?

Why are some animals only found in certain parts of the world?

Many animals, such as sparrows, beetles and rats, are found in every continent. They can fly, or have been carried on boats. They all eat a variety of foods, and can cope with different climates. Other animals are only found in certain areas. Here are three reasons why.

The three-toed sloth eats cecropia tree leaves, found in South American forests.

The polar bear's thick fur coat suits a cold environment.

The kangaroos of Australia could live elsewhere. The ocean between Australia and the rest of the world prevents them from travelling.

1. They only eat food found in the area they live in.

2. They can only live within a certain range of temperatures.

3. They cannot travel long distances because of barriers like oceans or mountains.

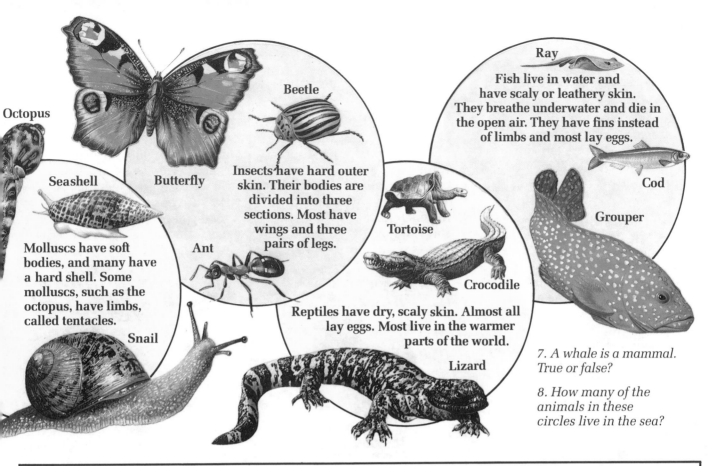

Octopus

Seashell

Butterfly

Beetle

Ant

Molluscs have soft bodies, and many have a hard shell. Some molluscs, such as the octopus, have limbs, called tentacles.

Insects have hard outer skin. Their bodies are divided into three sections. Most have wings and three pairs of legs.

Snail

Tortoise

Crocodile

Lizard

Reptiles have dry, scaly skin. Almost all lay eggs. Most live in the warmer parts of the world.

Ray

Fish live in water and have scaly or leathery skin. They breathe underwater and die in the open air. They have fins instead of limbs and most lay eggs.

Cod

Grouper

7. A whale is a mammal. True or false?

8. How many of the animals in these circles live in the sea?

How do animals fit into their environment?

Animal species can change their appearance and behavior to fit their environment. This can take thousands of years, and is called evolution. Here you can see how two different sorts of fish have evolved to fit into two completely different kinds of environment.

Tall, narrow bodies help angelfish shelter in coral reefs.

Muscular bodies help barracuda swim huge distances in the ocean.

9. Which one of these is a fish: a) starfish; b) dolphin; c) salmon?

10. Which scientist first suggested the theory of evolution: a) Charles Darwin; b) Galileo; c) Isaac Newton?

Did you know?

Three-quarters of all known animal species are insects. A third of all known insect species are beetles.

11. Which one of these is not an insect: a) moth; b) termite; c) iguana; d) locust?

What are food chains?

All animals need to eat plants or other animals to give them energy to survive. Plant-eating animals, called herbivores, are eaten by meat-eating animals (carnivores). These may be eaten in turn by other carnivores. This sequence is called a food chain. Within the chain, energy from food passes from one living thing to another. An animal that hunts another animal is called a predator. The animal that is hunted is called prey.

Here is a simple food chain, showing who eats who.

Plant

Greenfly

Blue tit

Domestic cat

12. Is a lion a carnivore or a herbivore?

13. When one kind of animal dies out this is called: a) extinction; b) exhaustion; c) exhibitionism.

14. The Ancient Egyptians worshipped cats. True or false?

15. Can you put this food chain in the right order? thrush caterpillar fox cabbage

Animal families

Apart from staying alive, producing the next generation is an animal's strongest instinct. These two pages look at how animals care for their young.

How many babies do animals have?

The number of eggs or babies that an animal has depends on the type of animal. The giant clam makes millions of eggs every year. Most are eaten by other animals but a few may survive. The sperm whale, though, only has one baby every three or four years.

The clam releases millions of eggs into the water around it.

The clam does nothing to look after its offspring. The whale, on the other hand, provides its calf with milk for at least two years.

Sperm whale

1. Put these animals in order of size: a) elephant; b) sperm whale; c) giant clam.

How do penguins hatch their eggs?

In order to hatch, birds' eggs need warmth. In Antarctica, the male emperor penguin warms an egg by perching it on its feet under a fold of skin. This keeps it away from the frozen ground. The penguin stays still over the egg for eight weeks waiting for it to hatch.

Emperor penguin

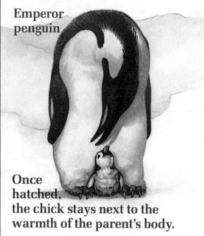

Once hatched, the chick stays next to the warmth of the parent's body.

2. Warming an egg to hatch it is called: a) incineration; b) invitation; c) incubation.

Young penguins too big to shelter under their parents, huddle together to keep warm.

3. What do penguins eat?

4. Penguins fly north for the winter. True or false?

Why do baby animals look different from adults?

Some young animals have different body coverings from the parents. Ducklings, for example, are covered with soft, brown feathers called down. Down keeps them warm and is good camouflage. As they get older, they grow stiffer feathers which help them to fly.

5. Which is bigger, a duck's egg or a hen's egg?

A young emperor angelfish looks very different from an adult. This is to stop an adult from mistaking it for a rival for food and mates, and fighting it.

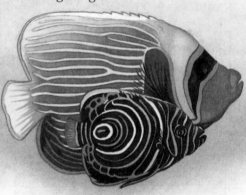

6. Which one of these is not a real fish: a) angelfish; b) butterflyfish; c) flying fish; d) rocket fish?

How does a young gorilla learn gorilla manners?

Gorillas live in large groups. While they are growing up they learn how to get on with their group. They become adults when they are between seven and ten years old.

Pretend fights show who is stronger and who to treat with respect.

8. Are gorillas carnivores or herbivores?

This young gorilla is practicing its grooming skills, removing dirt and insects from the other gorilla's fur.

The baby learns by watching everything the mother does.

7. Gorillas beat their chests: a) to make themselves cough; b) to look threatening; c) to crush fleas.

How do animals shelter their young?

Some animals build a nest or den for their young to keep them safe. Many birds, for instance, build nests high up in trees, or on cliff ledges.

9. Which bird lays its egg in another bird's nest?

Polar bears build a den under the snow for their cubs.

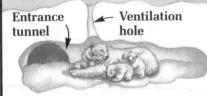

Entrance tunnel   **Ventilation hole**

Kangaroos carry their young in a pouch – a sort of built-in nest.

10. Kangaroos are only found in one continent. Which one?

Did you know?

The female praying mantis eats her mate. This provides her with energy to lay eggs.

Where does a crocodile lay its eggs?

Crocodiles lay their eggs in a nest of plants near the river bank and cover them with mud. The mother stands guard over them. The baby crocodiles make squeaking noises to let the mother know they have hatched. She breaks into the nest, and takes them in her mouth to the river, where they are safer from predators.

11. Crocodiles cover their eggs with mud; a) to hide them; b) to keep them warm; c) to stop them from breaking.

12. A Korean circus once taught a couple of crocodiles to waltz. True or false?

Why might a scorpion eat her young?

Scorpions are very aggressive meat-eaters. If they are hungry they may even eat their young. They can produce another large brood very easily.

Scorpions carry their young on their backs.

13. Baby scorpions sometimes eat each other. True or false?

Are queen bees different from other bees?

Although thousands of bees live together, only one bee, called a queen, lays eggs. Male bees, called drones, mate with the queen. Female bees, called workers, look after the eggs.

14. Honeybees show other bees where to find food by: a) dancing; b) singing; c) buzzing.

15. What are these cells made of?

The queen bee lays eggs in these cells.

Queen

Worker

Staying alive

These two pages look at how some animals hunt, and how other animals avoid being eaten.

What makes a good hunter?

The Indian tiger, like all tigers, has the abilities a good hunter needs. It has speed, strength, sharp senses and a talent for moving silently. Its skills and senses enable it to catch all kinds of animals, from young elephants to birds. Many of its features are found in other meat-eating animals.

Camouflage stripes make the tiger almost invisible in long grass.

Over short distances, the tiger can run as fast as antelope and deer, its swiftest prey.

1. Tigers can hide in grass as short as 2ft (60cm). True or false?

2. The tiger's favourite food is: a) wild pig; b) potatoes; c) people.

The body is flexible enough to run, pounce and crawl. The tiger can climb trees to catch birds and monkeys.

Good hearing, sight and smell help find prey.

The strong jaw can kill in a single bite.

Sharp claws come out when the tiger attacks.

Why do some animals hunt in packs?

Some animals, such as wolves, hunt in packs because it enables them to attack prey bigger and stronger than themselves. They are also likely to catch more food. They have to share their catch with the rest of the pack.

Other animals, such as leopards, hunt alone. They only attack smaller or weaker prey. However, when they do catch anything they do not have to share it with other animals.

3. Where do leopards usually hide their prey after they have killed it?

4. Which of these animals is the wolf's nearest animal relative: a) tiger; b) rat; c) poodle?

5. Which one of these animals hunts in a pack: a) harpy eagle; b) lion; c) giant anteater?

How do animals hunt their prey?

Hunters who are not especially strong or fast have to use special tricks to get close enough to their prey to catch them. Here are some examples.

Some animals, such as moray eels, hide themselves and lie in wait for their prey.

Moray eel

6. A moray eel can grow to: a) 3.3ft (1m); b) 10ft (3m); c) 100ft (30m).

Some animals, like this heron, use bait to attract prey.

The heron waves a feather which a fish might mistake for a fly.

7. What do you think the angler fish does with this?

Animals that move slower than their prey might use a trap. Many spiders weave a sticky web to catch insects.

8. Spiders eat their webs. True or false?

Some animals have their own weapons. The chameleon has a sticky tongue curled up inside its mouth which shoots out to capture insects.

9. The chameleon can change color to suit its surroundings. True or false?

How do animals protect themselves?

Animals only fight to defend themselves as a last resort. Here are some of the ways in which animals try to escape from predators.

Camouflage coloring helps an animal blend in with its environment. Some animals, like the sole, can even change color to match their surroundings.

10. If a sole is placed on a chess board it will match the squares. True or false?

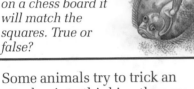

Some animals try to trick an attacker into thinking they are more dangerous than they really are.

Cats fluff up their fur to look bigger.

The Io moth has a pattern like a frightening face on its wings.

Animals that sting, such as bees and wasps, inject poison into an enemy.

11. Bees die if they sting. True or false?

Some animals offer a part of themselves to eat. They hope this will distract an attacker, and also satisfy its appetite.

12. Which of these animals can break off a part of itself: a) parrot; b) lizard; c) donkey?

If starfish are attacked they can shed an arm. A new one will grow.

How do animals avoid attack?

The size and strength of large animals like elephants make them difficult to kill. Most smaller animals avoid danger by hiding or running away. Healthy animals are seldom caught. It is usually the old, very young, sick or injured who are eaten. They are too slow to escape.

Like many plant-eaters, deer gather in herds. They are safer in groups than on their own.

Newborn deer can walk almost immediately. This helps them stay with their herd.

13. What are baby deer called?

Over long distances, the deer can outrun most attackers. The feet can be used to kick if the deer is cornered.

14. Which one of these is not a type of deer: a) caribou; b) elk; c) llama?

Spotted deer are good at defending themselves. They have certain features, found in many plant-eating animals, which help them escape from hunters.

Antlers can jab an attacker.

Good sight and hearing alert the deer to danger.

Male spotted deer →

The long neck gives a good view of the surroundings.

Female spotted deer

Spotted camouflage helps hide the deer in grass and forest.

How can bright colors protect an animal?

Some small animals, such as this cinnabar caterpillar, have bright colors to warn hunters that they are poisonous and taste horrible.

15. What do caterpillars turn into?

Did you know?

Some crabs defend themselves by placing sea anemones, which have stinging tentacles, on their claws.

Northern forest animals

Much of the land in the far north of the world is covered with forest. These forests, shown in white on the map, almost circle the earth.

The forest provides animals with a shield from harsh Arctic winds, and a good supply of food – at least in the warmer months. Compared with other parts of the world, though, there are few animals here, especially in the winter.

1. Which three continents contain northern forests?

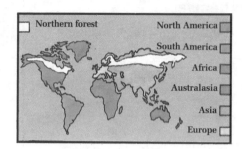

Northern forest
North America
South America
Africa
Australasia
Asia
Europe

How do animals survive the winter?

In the winter the forest is covered with snow and the temperature can drop to −40°F (−40°C). There is little to eat and it is difficult for the animals of the forest to keep themselves warm.

Lynx

In the winter a lynx may have to hunt over an area of 80 square miles (200 square kilometers) to find enough food to stay alive.

2. Why have humans hunted the lynx in the past?

3. Which one of the animals on this page is named after a type of tree found in the northern forest?

Moose

The moose eats as much as it can in the summer. It stores this food as fat on its body, for the harsh winter months.

4. The moose is a type of deer. True or false?

Many of the smaller mammals, like this woodchuck, save their energy by hibernating (sleeping through the winter months).

Woodchuck

To survive without eating, the woodchuck slows its heartbeat from 80 beats a minute to four. Breathing drops from 28 breaths a minute to one.

Pine marten

The pine marten, like most northern forest mammals, has a thick fur coat to keep it warm.

5. Which of these is not a good spot to hibernate in: a) underground; b) hollow tree; c) cave; d) tree top?

What is the forest like in the spring and summer?

Spring brings great changes. Snow melts, trees and flowers bloom, and insect eggs hatch. Lemmings, voles and other small animals come out of hibernation and breed in great numbers.

When summer arrives, the forest is like an overflowing pantry. There is so much food that birds such as the wood warbler migrate from further south to spend the summer here.

Lemming

Wood warbler

6. Which one of these animals migrates: a) python; b) thrush; c) dormouse; d) oyster?

7. Which one of these animals is the lemming's greatest enemy: a) owl; b) vole; c) wood warbler?

Why do beavers build dams?

Beavers are found throughout the northern forests. They protect themselves from predators by building a large nest called a lodge and flooding the area around it. They do this by building a dam on a stream.

8. In which one of these countries would you find beavers: a) Chile; b) Italy; c) Canada?

9. Beavers build small canals to ferry logs to their dams. True or false?

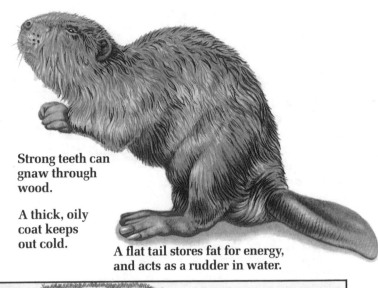

Strong teeth can gnaw through wood.

A thick, oily coat keeps out cold.

A flat tail stores fat for energy, and acts as a rudder in water.

The dam is made of wood, grass and mud. It keeps the entrance to the lodge underwater.

10. What do you think the lodge is made of?

11. Why is the entrance underwater?

A male and female beaver live here with their family.

How do bears bring up their cubs?

Bear cubs stay with their mother for two years. She protects them fiercely and teaches them what to eat. Bears are not normally friendly with each other, but bear mothers sometimes babysit for other bears. They may even adopt another mother bear's cubs if the mother dies.

Bears stand up to get a better view of their surroundings.

Bear cubs learn hunting skills by watching their mother.

12. Bears build igloos to shelter in during the winter. True or false?

13. These bears are: a) koala bears; b) grizzly bears; c) Himalayan bears; d) polar bears.

14. Which one of these games have humans taught bears to play: a) ice hockey; b) hopscotch; c) Scrabble?

15. A bear can eat 200,000 berries in a single day. True or false?

Bears love to eat salmon, which they catch with their paws.

Did you know?

In the forests of northern Japan, volcanic springs form pools full of hot water. Macaque monkeys can keep themselves warm in the cold winter by soaking in these pools.

Why is it dangerous to feed bears?

Bears love the food humans eat. Once they have tasted it they may venture into campsites and towns looking for more. Many bears that do this are shot as they can be dangerous.

Rainforest animals

Because most rainforests are hot and damp, the trees and plants that grow in them are the biggest in the world. These forests provide so much food and shelter that far more animals live here than in most other environments.

Most of the animals shown here come from South America, which has the largest single forest in the world. Rainforests are shown in white on the map.

1. Which continent on this map does not have a rainforest?

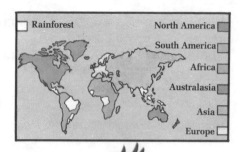

Rainforest · North America · South America · Africa · Australasia · Asia · Europe

What do rainforests look like?

Rainforests have four main layers.

At the top are the tallest trees, called "emergents."

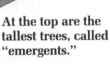

The tops of other trees form a roof, or "canopy," to the forest.

Beneath the canopy is another layer of trees.

The final layer is the forest floor.

Who lives at the top?

Birds and the lightest, most agile climbers live at the top of the forest. Harpy eagles live here. They eat other birds and small mammals. Many animals stay away from this level to avoid them.

2. This harpy eagle could carry off a monkey. True or false?

Are sloths really lazy?

Sloths do everything very slowly. The leaves they eat take a long time to digest and convert into energy, so they need to save their strength. They sleep often and hang motionless for hours when awake.

Sloths come down from the trees once a week to excrete. This is when they are most likely to be attacked and eaten.

3. Jaguars find sleeping sloths by listening for them snoring. True or false?

4. How many hours a day do sloths sleep: a) 3; b) 15 to 18; c) over 24?

Strong claws grip the branches.

Tiny green plants called algae grow over their fur. This helps to camouflage them. Moths often live in the fur.

The fur grows from stomach to back. This lets rain drip off easily.

Who lives at the bottom?

Animals that cannot fly or climb live on the forest floor. Capybaras, tapirs and millions of insects live here.

Jaguars hide in low branches and drop on their prey. They eat tapirs and other plant-eaters.

5. Jaguars don't hunt at the top of trees because they are afraid of: a) heights; b) harpy eagles; c) breaking thinner branches.

The capybara is over 3ft (1m) long. Capybaras are rodents, like rats and squirrels.

The tapir is a shy plant-eater which only comes out at night. It picks up food with its trunk.

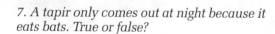

6. The capybara is the largest rodent in the world. True or false?

7. A tapir only comes out at night because it eats bats. True or false?

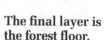

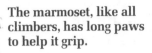

How are animals suited to life in the trees?

Most animals that live in the forest can either fly or climb.

The parrot's short, broad wings help it fly through the gaps between trees and branches.

8. What sort of food do parrots eat?

9. Which is not a type of parrot: a) cockatoo; b) parakeet; c) macaw; d) condor?

The marmoset, like all climbers, has long paws to help it grip.

10. Which two rainforest animals on these two pages is the marmoset most similar to?

11. A marmoset is about the size of a kitten. True or false?

The spider monkey has a flexible tail which can grasp branches.

How can animals fly without wings?

Some rainforest animals in Africa and Asia have body shapes which help them glide between trees.

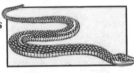

Gliding snakes flatten their bodies in flight.

Flying frogs have large webbed feet for gliding.

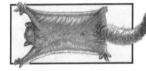

Flying squirrels have large skin flaps.

Did you know?

The arrow-poison frog is so venomous that some South American tribes dip arrows into the poison to make them more deadly. A frog 1in (2.5cm) long makes poison for 50 arrows.

Why is the rainforest so noisy?

Many rainforest animals claim an area for themselves. They make a lot of noise to warn others to keep away from their territory.

How big is an army of army ants?

When army ants go out looking for food, up to 200,000 of them march in a column 66ft (20m) wide. They move at about 46ft (14m) per hour, capturing spiders, cockroaches, scorpions and ants.

12. Do army ants move quicker than a sloth?

13. Do people live in the rainforest?

Howler monkeys make an eerie howling noise every morning and evening.

14. The sound of a howler monkey's howl travels: a) 0.6 miles (1km); b) 3 miles (5km); c) 10 miles (16km).

15. Which one is the quietest: a) spider monkey; b) tapir; c) parrot?

City wildlife

Ever since towns and cities were first built 8,000 years ago, wild animals have lived in them. The city provides two things that all animals need: plenty of food and shelter.

What sort of animals live in the city?

City animals need to be tough enough to stand noise, pollution and bustle. They have to be able to live close to people and eat a variety of foods. They need to breed easily and make use of all kinds of available space for shelter.

City trash cans provide food for foxes.

Rats and mice live wherever food is stored or left out. Rats can live almost anywhere, even in sewers, but mice prefer warmer places. Rats are tough and can eat many kinds of food, including meat. They can breed at an alarming rate.

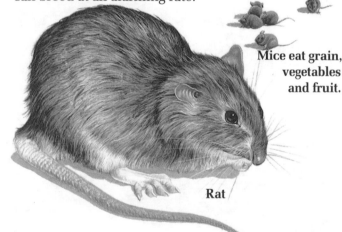

Mice eat grain, vegetables and fruit.

Rat

Bats live in caves in the wild. Attics and towers provide similar shelter in cities.

Pigeon

Pigeons have evolved from seashore birds that nest in cliffs. They feel at home sheltering in the nooks and crannies of tall buildings.

1. Which one of the animals on this page did the legendary Pied Piper drive out of the town of Hamelin?

Insects like silverfish, houseflies and cockroaches compete with each other for food and shelter.

House fly

2. Which one of these is not a real insect: a) clothes moth; b) tile termite; c) furniture beetle?

3. How long does a fly live: a) ten hours; b) ten days; c) ten weeks?

4. Mice grow up to be rats. True or false?

5. A female rat can have twelve babies every: a) twenty minutes; b) eight weeks; c) two years.

6. Which animal shown on this page is seen the most in cities?

Did you know?

Termites that live in the city will eat anything – even plastic-coated wiring which has no food value at all. Nobody knows why they do this.

Why don't more animals live in the city?

Many animals are unsuited to the food and shelter the city provides.

Here are some of the reasons why not all animals can live in the city.

An animal such as the hippopotamus would be too large to find shelter in the city. Foxes are usually the biggest city animals. 	**Some animals cannot find the food that they need in a city. Pandas, for example, can only eat bamboo, which they find in the forests of western China.** 	**Some animals, such as deer, are too timid to live in the crowded, noisy city.** 
Animals large and fierce enough to attack and eat humans, like this tiger, would be killed if they came into a city to look for food. 	**Some animals cannot live with the noise, smoke, fumes and dirty water of the city. This butterflyfish needs clean, clear water in which to live.** 	*7. How many of these reasons would apply to this crocodile?* 

The night shift

As day changes to night, most animals retire to their nests and burrows. Nighttime (or nocturnal) creatures take their

places and share their space and food. Instead of hawks there are owls. Instead of butterflies there are moths.

How do animals see in the dark?

Many nocturnal animals have fine hearing, or large eyes that can see very well in the dark.

Owls are one of the few types of bird that hunt at night. Owl eyes are a hundred times sharper than human eyes. Owls can spot a mouse by candlelight 300ft (91m) away. They also have excellent hearing to help them find prey.

8. Owls cannot move their eyes in their heads. True or false?

Bats are such successful hunters that one in four mammals on Earth is a bat. They hunt with their own unique animal radar system.

Bats make high pitched clicking sounds. Their big ears pick up the echoes these clicks make. The echoes tell the bat what the countryside looks like and where its prey can be found.

How do bats tell the clicks from the echoes?

So they are not confused by too much sound, bats' ears "switch off" when the click is made. They "switch on" a millisecond later to listen to the echo.

9. Do vampire bats really exist?

10. Bats can pick up radio signals. True or false?

How do glowworms glow?

Glowworms and fireflies light up at night. Two chemicals in the tail react together to produce a cold yellow-green light. Despite being so visible, they are rarely eaten by predators because they taste horrible.

11. The glowworm glows to: a) read at night; b) attract a mate; c) light the way for other animals.

12. Which one of these is not a night-time animal: a) hedgehog; b) mouse; c) eagle; d) potto; e) nightingale?

Why do some animals only come out at night?

Fewer animals are around at night so there is less competition for food. This suits small and timid animals like this African potto.

13. The potto is a type of: a) lion; b) loris; c) lizard.

Most predators hunt during the day. Animals such as this mole, which is almost blind, have less chance of being eaten at night.

14. Where do moles make their homes?

In very hot parts of the world, the heat of the day is tiring. This kangaroo rat comes out at night when it is cooler.

Did you know?

Some frogs and toads do not mind the taste of glowworms. Sometimes they eat so many they are lit up from inside.

15. In some countries fireflies are put in lanterns and used for lighting. True or false?

13

The open ocean

The oceans take up 71% of the world's surface. The earth's first creatures lived here 3,500 million years ago. Now the oceans are home to a huge variety of animals.

Some areas of the sea are as different from each other as rainforest and desert. Surface winds, light, depth, currents and temperature all affect the amount of life in the sea. This map shows in white which areas of the ocean are the richest in life.

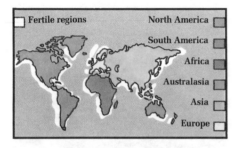

| Fertile regions | North America ☐ |
| South America ☐ |
| Africa ☐ |
| Australasia ☐ |
| Asia ☐ |
| Europe ☐ |

1. What do the most fertile regions of the sea have in common?

2. Which is the biggest ocean?

How do fish breathe underwater?

Fish suck water over rows of feather-like gills, at the back of their mouths.

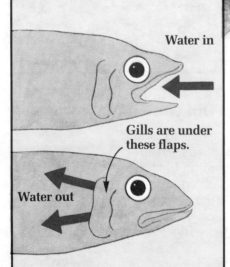

Water in

Gills are under these flaps.

Water out

A fish's gills filter oxygen from the water in a similar way to how our lungs take oxygen from the air.

Who lives in the sea?

Along with fish, animals of almost every type can be found in the sea. On this page are some of the main ones.

Most fish, such as these cod, have bones and shiny scales. The scales overlap and form a flexible, streamlined skin.

Some fish, like the shark, have soft, rubbery skeletons and scales as rough as sandpaper. Fish like these lived in the sea before dinosaurs existed.

Crustaceans like this lobster have hard shells and legs. Shrimps and crabs are also crustaceans.

A few reptiles, like this turtle, live in the sea.

Some birds, like this cormorant, can dive underwater to hunt for fish.

Mammals like this sea lion, and seals and whales, also live in the sea. They cannot breathe underwater but can hold their breath for a long time.

3. A group of birds is called a flock. What is a group of fish called?

4. Fish sleep: a) upside down; b) in a glassy-eyed trance; c) lying on the sea bottom with a pebble as a pillow.

5. Which one of these is a crustacean: a) pangolin; b) piddock; c) prawn; d) piranha?

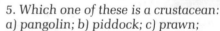

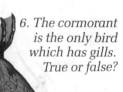

6. The cormorant is the only bird which has gills. True or false?

7. Which of these birds is not a good swimmer: a) penguin; b) petrel; c) puffin; d) parrot?

Why do whales leap?

Some whales occasionally leap out of the water, landing with an immense splash. No one knows for certain why they do it. The following reasons have been suggested:

1. To communicate with other whales. The sound of the splash travels far.

2. To let the whale see further than it can at sea level.

3. To shake off little creatures which live on the whale's skin.

Humpback whale

8. Do you know what this sort of leaping is called?

9. What sort of animals live on whales: a) jellyfish; b) barnacles; c) sharks?

10. When whales give birth, how many calves do they usually have?

What is plankton?

Any sea creature that drifts with the tides and currents instead of swimming, is called plankton. Most plankton are microscopic, but some, like jellyfish, can be quite large. There are two main types of plankton, called phytoplankton and zooplankton.

Phytoplankton are tiny plants. They need light to live, so they are found in the top, sunlit layers of the ocean. They provide food for many different animals.

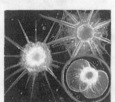

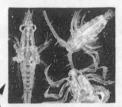

Zooplankton are animals. They eat each other and phytoplankton. Many are minute crustaceans or newly hatched eggs.

12. Are herring plankton?

Phytoplankton magnified thousands of times. ➘

Zooplankton magnified hundreds of times.

11. 1.3 cubic yards (A cubic meter) of seawater can contain 200,000 plankton. True or false?

13. Plankton is a Greek word that means: a) wanderer; b) sea food; c) microscope?

Why do deep sea fish look so extraordinary?

Deeper in the ocean it is very cold, and below 1,970ft (600m) it is pitch-black. Very little lives here so deep sea fish have to make the most of any chance they get to eat.

Over half the deep sea creatures can light up parts of their body. As well as a lure for prey, these lights are used to attract a mate in the total darkness.

14. What do you think this fish is called: a) a viper fish; b) a gobble fish; c) a fanged blemish?

15. The lights on deep sea fish are solar powered. True or false?

The mouth can be opened very wide by unhinging the bottom jaw. This enables the fish to eat large prey.

Luminous spots act as a lure for prey.

Curved, sharp teeth make it difficult for prey to escape.

Did you know?

Sharks have a row of teeth on a kind of conveyor belt in their bottom jaw. If they bite something tough and their teeth fall out, other teeth move up to replace them.

Life at the edge of the sea

The creatures that live at the edge of the sea are quite different from the animals of the ocean. Instead of open water, they live in mud, rock or coral. For those that live on the shore, the tide comes and goes twice a day, exposing them to both air and water.

Who lives on the beach?

At first glance it is difficult to tell if anything other than seabirds live on the beach. Plants rarely grow here. Only the occasional pattern in the sand gives a clue to the animal life under the surface.

The birds' beaks are various lengths. This lets them search for shells, worms and snails that live at different depths in the sand. They hunt for food right up to the water's edge.

1. Why do you think these birds all have long legs?

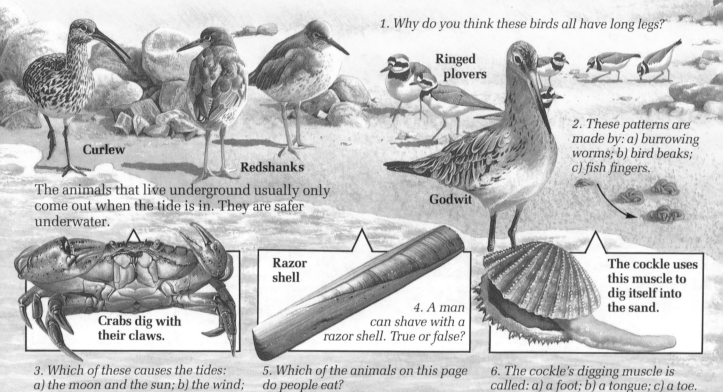

Curlew

Redshanks

Ringed plovers

Godwit

2. These patterns are made by: a) burrowing worms; b) bird beaks; c) fish fingers.

The animals that live underground usually only come out when the tide is in. They are safer underwater.

Crabs dig with their claws.

Razor shell

4. A man can shave with a razor shell. True or false?

The cockle uses this muscle to dig itself into the sand.

3. Which of these causes the tides: a) the moon and the sun; b) the wind; c) earthquakes; d) whales?

5. Which of the animals on this page do people eat?

6. The cockle's digging muscle is called: a) a foot; b) a tongue; c) a toe.

Who lives on the rocks?

Unlike shore animals who can burrow into the wet sand, rock dwellers have to sit out in the open when the tide goes out. They need water in order to breathe, so they will die if they dry out. At low tide, they save a supply of water inside their bodies or shells to prevent this.

The barnacle is protected by a tough shell.

A strong cement binds the barnacle to its perch.

Limpet

In the open air, crabs carry water to breathe inside their shells.

Rock goby

Anemone

Outside the water, the anemone can curl itself up. Its outside is tough and leathery to keep it from drying out.

A tight seal keeps water in.

The barnacle's tentacles wave in the water, picking up food.

Oyster

7. Barnacles also settle on the underside of: a) aircraft; b) ships; c) windsurfers.

8. Which one of these animals would you not find in a rockpool: a) sea urchin; b) starfish; c) salamander?

What are coral reefs?

Coral reefs are made up of millions of little animals called coral polyps. Their bodies have hard, bone-like cases and they live together in huge colonies. These reefs are the biggest animal-made structures on earth. The biggest reef, the Great Barrier Reef, stretches for more than 1,260 miles (2,000km).

Coral reefs are the most colorful and crowded underwater environments on earth. There is a good supply of food and the reef offers many caves and crevices for shelter.

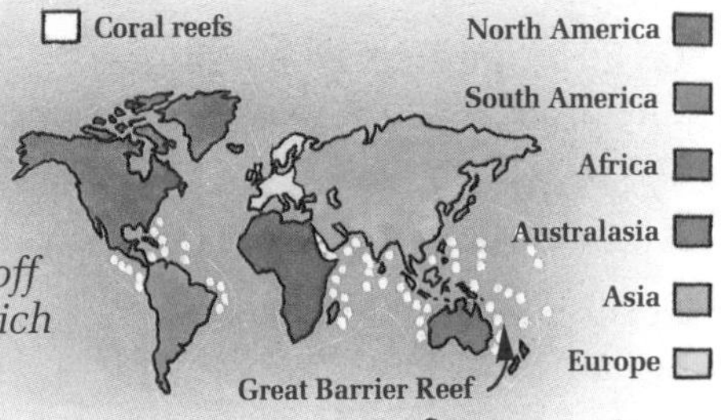

Who lives on the reef?

An extraordinary number of different sea creatures live on the coral reef. Most of them are brightly colored to help blend in with their equally colorful environment. This also helps them recognize their own kind from all the other animals that share their environment.

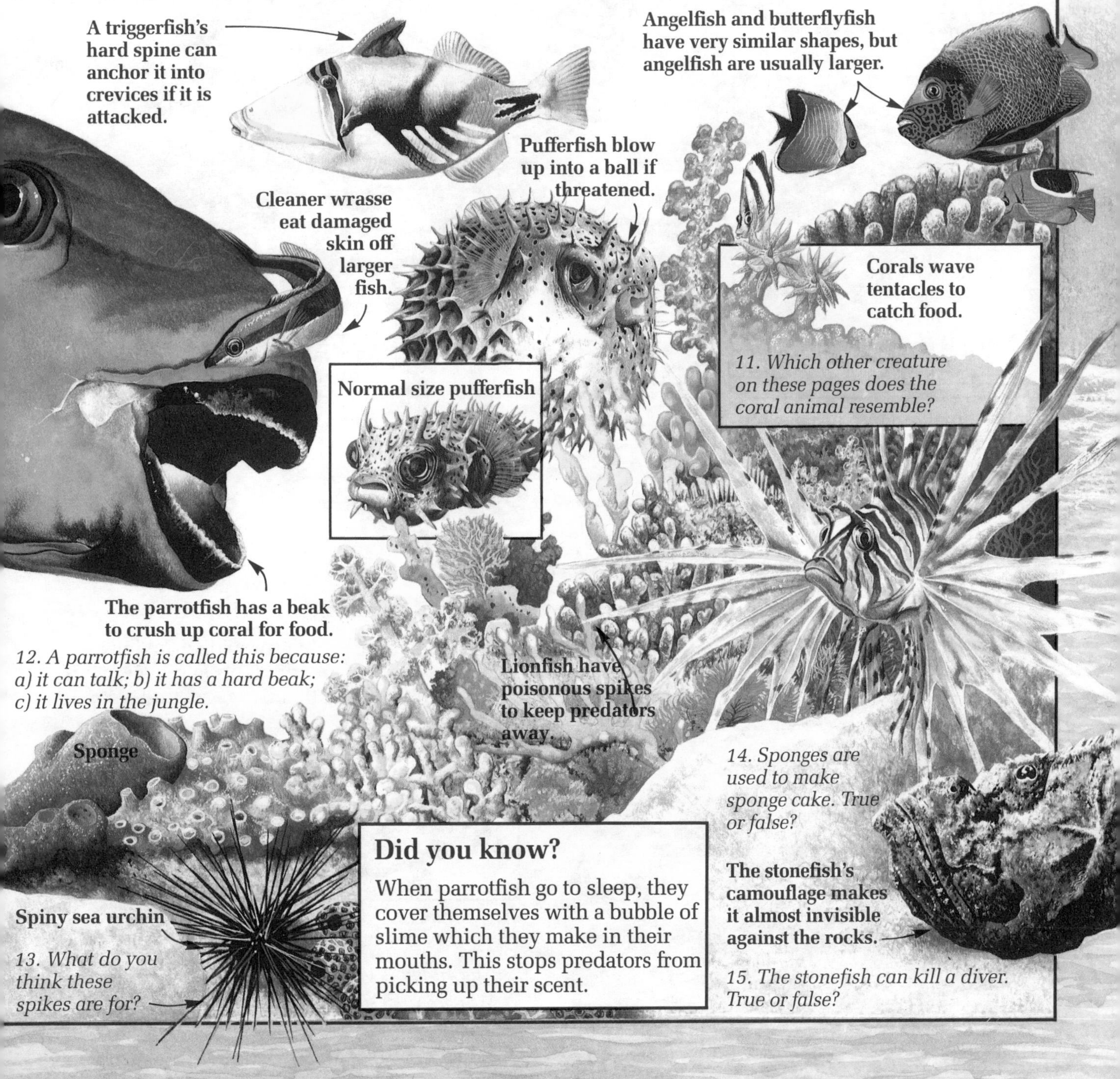

Where are coral reefs found?

Reefs are found in warm, clear, shallow waters off tropical coastlines and islands. Corals need warmth and sunlight to grow.

☐ Coral reefs

North America ■
South America ■
Africa ■
Australasia ■
Asia ☐
Europe ☐

Great Barrier Reef

9. Are there coral reefs in Europe?

10. The Great Barrier Reef is off the coast of which country?

A triggerfish's hard spine can anchor it into crevices if it is attacked.

Angelfish and butterflyfish have very similar shapes, but angelfish are usually larger.

Cleaner wrasse eat damaged skin off larger fish.

Pufferfish blow up into a ball if threatened.

Normal size pufferfish

Corals wave tentacles to catch food.

11. Which other creature on these pages does the coral animal resemble?

The parrotfish has a beak to crush up coral for food.

12. A parrotfish is called this because: a) it can talk; b) it has a hard beak; c) it lives in the jungle.

Lionfish have poisonous spikes to keep predators away.

Sponge

14. Sponges are used to make sponge cake. True or false?

Spiny sea urchin

13. What do you think these spikes are for?

Did you know?

When parrotfish go to sleep, they cover themselves with a bubble of slime which they make in their mouths. This stops predators from picking up their scent.

The stonefish's camouflage makes it almost invisible against the rocks.

15. The stonefish can kill a diver. True or false?

Living without water

The deserts of the world are wastelands of rock, rubble and sand. Scorching hot by day and bitterly cold by night, they have almost no water.

The largest desert is the Sahara, which stretches from northern Africa into Asia. The map on the right shows where deserts are found.

1. Which of these is not a desert: a) Gobi; b) Kalahari; c) Namib; d)Kenya?

2. Which continent on this map does not have a desert?

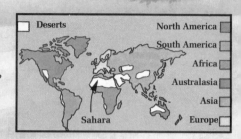

Deserts

North America

South America

Africa

Australasia

Asia

Sahara

Europe

How do animals survive in the desert?

Desert animals cope with sand and lack of water in a variety of ways. The camel is especially well suited to life in the desert.

In the same way that a large pan of water takes longer to boil than a small one, a large animal like the camel stays cooler in the heat than a small one.

Animals like this gerbil shelter from the sun in burrows.

Animals like this desert hedgehog come out at night when it is cooler.

Many small mammals have big ears, like this fennec fox. These provide a large surface for heat to escape from, in the same way that soup cools quicker on a plate than in a mug.

Hairy ears and eye lashes, and slit nostrils keep out dust and sand.

3. The hump stores: a) water; b) fat; c) fuel.

An insulating wool coat keeps out both the heat of day and the cold of night.

Wide feet stop the camel from sinking into the sand.

4. Camels with one hump are called: a) dormitories; b) doubloons; c) dromedaries.

5. A camel can drink 20gal (90l) in one ten-minute drink. True or false?

How do animals move in the desert?

Sand is very tiring to walk on. It can also be scalding hot. Desert animals cope with this in a variety of ways.

The sidewinder snake winds itself along. Only a very small part of its body touches the sand at any one time.

Jerboas take large leaps over the sand.

Where do animals find water?

Rare streams and springs provide drinking water and create fertile areas of plants and trees. Most animals though find their water in food.

6. What are the fertile parts of the desert called?

The Gila monster reptile finds its water from the animals that it eats.

The addax gets all of its water from the plants and grasses in the desert.

7. The addax never needs to drink. True or false?

8. Which is a desert plant: a) daffodil; b) cactus; c) bamboo.

Living at the ends of the earth

The Arctic and the Antarctic are the coldest places on earth. Very few kinds of animals live here, but those that do can be found in large numbers.

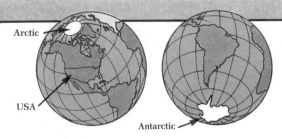

Arctic

USA

Antarctic

What is the Arctic like?

The most northern part of the world is covered with a great frozen sea—the Arctic Ocean. It is a bleak place. Even in midsummer the temperature rarely rises above 50°F (10°C).

9. What is the central point of the Arctic known as?

Who lives in the Arctic?

The polar bear is the biggest land animal of the Arctic. It is a strong swimmer and hunts seals. The polar bear only lives in this part of the world.

Arctic foxes often follow bears around, eating the food they leave.

Polar bear

Seals leave a breathing hole in the ice.

Fur under the paws gives a good grip on ice and keeps the feet warm.

Did you know?

In severe snow storms, polar bears scoop out shallow hollows in the snow. They sleep in them until the storm is over.

10. Can you name any other type of bear?

Many seabirds come for the summer, when sea food is plentiful.

The walrus is the only animal the polar bear fears. It usually eats fish and shellfish, but it is powerful enough to kill a bear.

What is the Antarctic like?

The Antarctic is a huge island, which is one and a half times the size of the USA. Two thirds of Antarctica has been covered with ice for the last four million years.

11. Is the Antarctic bigger than Africa?

Who lives in the Antarctic?

Most animal life is found around the coast, which is the warmest part of the Antarctic. The sea here is full of life and supports vast colonies of penguins and seals. Inland, only a few insects can survive the intense cold.

12. Ninety-five percent of the world's ice is found in the Antarctic. True or False?

Seals live in seas all over the world, but penguins only live on the coasts of countries in the far south.

The Weddell seal can stay underwater for an hour. When it dives, the heart slows down and oxygen only goes to the most vital body organs.

13. Seals are: a) mammals; b) fish; c) reptiles.

The leopard seal hunts penguins.

Are penguins birds?

Penguins are birds that have lost the ability to fly. Instead they have become superb swimmers.

14. Which one of these birds can fly: a) emu; b) kiwi; c) flamingo; d) penguin?

A layer of fat keeps out cold.

Wings act as flippers.

15. Do polar bears eat penguins?

Grassland wildlife

Grasslands (shown in white on the map) are found inland in some hot, dry countries. The countryside is covered in sturdy, long grasses. All the animals shown on these pages, apart from the South American anteater, are found in the vast, open plains of East Africa.

Lions, leopards and cheetahs hunt here, but animals are more likely to die of thirst, hunger or bush fires. They are also in danger from human hunters.

Rhinoceroses, for example, are killed for their horn. Some people believe it has magical powers even though it is made of the same substance as fingernails.

1. A rhino uses its horn to: a) burrow underground; b) scratch its back; c) attack its enemies.

2. The horn of a rhinoceros is made from: a) keratin; b) kerosine; c) korma.

Map legend:
- Grasslands
- North America
- South America
- Africa
- Australasia
- Asia
- Europe

Why do so many wild animals live here?

People have not been able to farm this land because it is too hot and dry for farm animals and crops.

There is usually plenty of suitable food for the wild animals that live here, though.

Elephant and giraffe feed on tree leaves.

Wildebeest and zebra graze on the grasses.

The leopard and lion are meat-eaters.

Vultures eat what the hunters leave.

3. Animals that eat plants are called herbivores. What are animals that eat other animals called?

4. How many kinds of animals on this page eat plants?

5. A zebra has black and white stripes: a) because it is a cross between a black horse and a white horse; b) for camouflage; c) because it is black currant and vanilla flavored.

Why do many animals go around in large groups?

Grass-eating animals like the wildebeest and zebra are safest in large groups, or herds. This confuses predators because so many targets make it difficult to decide which one to pick.

Strong animals can shelter weak or very young ones in the herd.

Some animals in the herd can graze while others keep a look out for danger.

Predators such as lions hunt more successfully in groups. They work together to create diversions and ambushes, and share a feast rather than squabble over it.

Herds of up to 10,000 wildebeest travel long distances overland in search of food.

6. Zebra foals can stand and walk within an hour of being born. True or false?

7. Which word is used to describe animals that travel long distances?

8. If lions and tigers mate, their cubs are called tigons or ligers. True or false?

Why do termites build huge mounds?

Termites need a lot of moisture. They cannot survive in the dry heat of the plains so they create a home that suits them better.

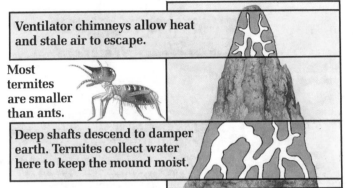

Ventilator chimneys allow heat and stale air to escape.

Most termites are smaller than ants.

Deep shafts descend to damper earth. Termites collect water here to keep the mound moist.

9. What do you think these mounds are made of: a) mushrooms; b) moss; c) mud?

How does an anteater eat?

This South American giant anteater sticks its nose into ants' nests and termite mounds. Its long, sticky tongue shoots out of its mouth at up to 160 times a minute. In this way it can eat up to 30,000 insects a day.

Powerful claws smash a hole in the nest.

10. The giant anteater's greatest enemy is the lion. True or false?

11. An anteater has a large, bushy tail: a) to help it keep warm; b) to sweep its den; c) to hide behind when it is frightened.

Why are elephants and giraffes so big?

An elephant eats twigs, leaves and bark which are difficult to digest. It needs a huge stomach to do this, so its body is big to hold it.

Giraffes' long necks enable them to eat leaves that other sorts of animals cannot reach.

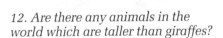

12. Are there any animals in the world which are taller than giraffes?

13. Which one of the animals on this page lives in a termitarium?

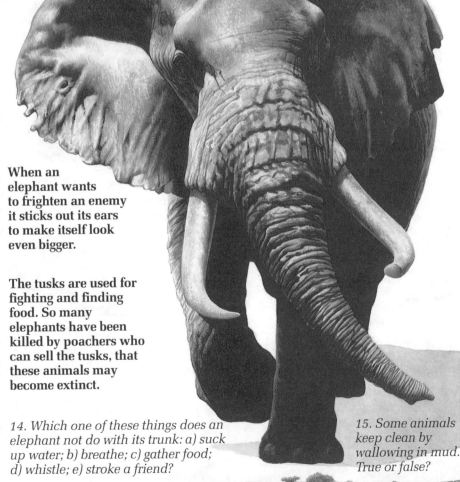

When an elephant wants to frighten an enemy it sticks out its ears to make itself look even bigger.

The tusks are used for fighting and finding food. So many elephants have been killed by poachers who can sell the tusks, that these animals may become extinct.

14. Which one of these things does an elephant not do with its trunk: a) suck up water; b) breathe; c) gather food; d) whistle; e) stroke a friend?

15. Some animals keep clean by wallowing in mud. True or false?

Did you know?

Despite being the heaviest land animals, elephants can move around almost silently. They have soft, elastic pads on their feet that muffle their footsteps.

Animal oddities

The shape of an animal's body helps it to survive. It enables it to cope with its environment and compete with other animals for food. The differences between animals help them all fit into their own particular environment.

These two pages look at some of the more unusual looking animals, and how their appearance helps them survive.

Why does the toucan have such a colorful bill?

These colors may help other toucans recognize their own kind among the many brightly-colored birds of the Amazon rainforest.

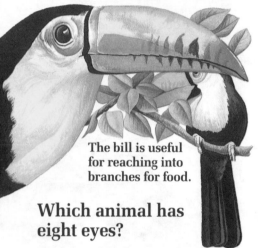

The bill is useful for reaching into branches for food.

Which animal has eight eyes?

Many spiders have eight eyes but they do not use them all at once. This jumping spider uses different sets of eyes as it stalks prey and then leaps on it.

These eyes detect movement from a distance.

These judge how far away insects are.

These eyes are used when the spider is stalking its prey.

1. Why should you be wary of the red back, funnelweb and black widow spider?

2. Some jumping spiders can leap more than 20 times their own body length. True or false?

Which thorns can move?

These African thorn bugs look like thorns on a branch. When they are still, it is difficult for their enemies to see them. Insects have copied many different shapes to stay hidden from predators.

3. Which one of these shapes is not copied by an insect: a) twig; b) bird dropping; c) red berry; d) snake head?

Why does the luminous jellyfish glow?

This jellyfish drifts in the ocean, coming to the surface at night where it glows softly in the dark water.

Jellyfish move very slowly. They cannot chase after food. The glow attracts prey, and other jellyfish to breed with.

The glow is made by tiny plant-like bacteria, which live in the jellyfish.

The tentacles have stings. They trap prey and discourage animals that may want to eat the jellyfish.

4. What do jellyfish have in common with sea anemones and corals?

5. Which one is not a jellyfish: a) aurelia; b) Portuguese man o' war; c) raspberry; d) purple sail?

Why is the pangolin covered with scales?

The pangolin's body is covered in hard, flat scales made of the same basic substance as your hair and fingernails. If it is attacked, it rolls up into an armored ball.

6. Which other animal in this book has a long sticky tongue and eats ants and termites?

7. Put these animals in order of size: pangolin, jumping spider, platypus, mudskipper.

The pangolin has no teeth. Instead it swallows stones to grind up the ants and termites it eats.

Its long sticky tongue is half the length of its body.

8. South Asian tribesmen make bagpipes out of the hollowed-out bodies of pangolins. True or false?

9. Which is the odd one out: a) rhino horn; b) fingernail; c) pangolin scale; d) elephant tusk?

Why are nudibranchs so colorful?

Gills for breathing.

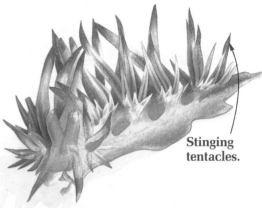

Stinging tentacles.

Many nudibranchs (pronounced new-dee-branks) have amazingly bright colors. This probably warns other sea animals not to eat them, as they are poisonous.

10. Which land animal is the nudibranch similar to?

One kind of nudibranch eats jellyfish and corals. It can transfer their stings from its stomach to its own tentacles and use them to defend itself.

What is a platypus?

The Australian platypus is a mammal that lays eggs. It feeds its young on milk (like all mammals) but this oozes out of its skin rather than from the nipples other mammals have.

The beak is covered by sensitive skin. It is used to find worms and shrimp in muddy water.

Webbed toes and a flat tail help it swim.

11. Young platypuses are called platykittens. True or false?

Did you know?

Two platypuses in the Bronx Zoo, New York, ate 25,000 worms a month, along with crayfish, frogs and egg custard. Despite only weighing 2-3lb (1-1.3kg) each, they cost more to feed than the zoo's elephants.

Can a fish survive out of water?

The mudskipper is one of the few fishes that can survive out of water. Like all fish it gets its oxygen from water rather than air. When it comes out of the sea it takes a supply of water along in a chamber inside its body. On land it skips about on muddy shores looking for food.

A chamber full of water, inside here, helps the mudskipper to breathe.

On land, the mudskipper uses these fins as legs.

Which fish shoots insects?

The archer fish of Southeast Asia shoots drops of water at insects. This knocks them off their perches into the water where they are eaten.

12. Archer fish can also knock birds off their perches. True or false?

13. Would you find the archer fish living in rivers or in oceans?

14. The air tank people use to breathe underwater is called: a) an aqualung; b) an aquarium; c) an aqueduct.

15. Male mudskippers attract females by: a) whistling; b) waving their back fin; c) doing somersaults.

Extraordinary animals

These pages look at animals who are able to do one particular thing better than any other animal.

These special abilities almost always help them find food or escape from being eaten.

Which animal has the strongest bite?

The great white shark almost certainly has the strongest bite. It attacks whales, dolphins, other sharks, and sometimes humans. It is about 26ft (8m) long. The jaw can bite down with a force equivalent to the weight of four elephants per tooth.

1. All sharks are dangerous to humans. True or false?

The shark's teeth point backwards to make it more difficult for prey to escape.

2. A shark's skin is covered with: a) leather; b) barbed scales; c) bone.

Which animal is the most indestructible?

The sponge is a very simple animal that lives in the sea. It eats by filtering food from the seawater that it sucks through its body. If parts of its body are broken off or eaten it can rebuild them. It is so indestructible that if it was broken up in a blender, it would still be able to put itself back together again.

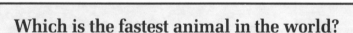

Which is the fastest animal in the world?

The fastest of all animals is the spine-tailed swift. It can fly at 106mph (170km/h).

Swifts spend most of their lives in the air, only landing to have their chicks. They can fly 560 miles (900km) in a single day.

The fastest animal in the sea is the sailfish. It can swim 68mph (109km/h). Its crescent-shaped tail is ideal for pushing it smoothly through the water.

The swift has a very streamlined shape and crescent-shaped wings.

12. What shape does the sailfish have in common with the spine-tailed swift?

10. Swifts can stay in the air for as long as two years. True or false?

11. What sort of food do you think swifts eat?

Other fast-swimming fish like the tuna and the swordfish also have crescent-shaped tails.

Which is the largest animal that ever lived?

The blue whale is the largest animal that ever lived. It is even bigger than the largest dinosaurs.

It has an average length of 100ft (30m) and weighs 132 tons (122 tonnes). The water supports its huge body.

4. The blue whale sings to other whales when: a) it is having a bath; b) it is happy; c) it wants to let them know where it is.

5. Do you know what blue whales eat?

Blue whale

African elephant, the largest land animal.

Brachiosaurus, the largest dinosaur.

Which is the most dangerous animal?

It is thought that mosquitoes have contributed to 50% of all natural human deaths since the beginning of recorded history. They pass on yellow fever and malaria when they feed on human blood.

6. Which of these eats mosquitoes: a) spider; b) snail; c) shark?

7. Which animal on these two pages might you use in your own bathroom?

Which is the greatest traveller?

The Arctic tern makes an annual journey of 24,000 miles (38,400 km) from the Arctic to the Antarctic and back. The tern breeds in the Arctic summer. Then it flies far south for the Antarctic summer, which is at the opposite time of the year. It probably does this because the food it eats is plentiful in polar summers.

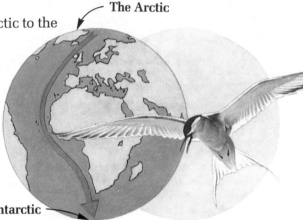

The Arctic

The Antarctic

8. The Arctic tern experiences more daylight than any other animal. True or false?

9. What sort of food does the Arctic tern travel to eat: a) crustaceans; b) polar bears; c) penguins?

---

13. Asian princes once trained cheetahs to catch antelope. True or false?

A very flexible backbone gives great power to the cheetah's legs.

Cheetahs are the fastest land animals. They can run at around 50mph (80km/h) but only for about 440 yd (400m). After a short chase they have to stop to cool down and catch their breath.

The cheetah is a medium-sized cat. It is only strong enough to catch small prey, most of which can run very fast. It has to be able to run even faster.

Claws act like spikes on running shoes. They give good grip and are especially useful for quick turns.

14. Put these cats in order of size: cheetah, domestic cat, lion, lynx.

15. Which of these is the slowest: a) snail; b) sloth; c) stonefish?

Long, light legs take huge strides.

Animal Megaquiz

All these questions are about animals that have appeared in Part One of this book. You can write your answers on a piece of paper and then check on page 32 to see how many you got right.

What do you know?

1. In which part of the world did life first appear millions of years ago?
2. Which one of these lived on Earth before the dinosaurs: a) shark; b) sheep; c) squirrel?
3. Which one of these birds swims well under water: a) cuckoo; b) crow: c) cormorant?
4. Which kind of animal can weigh 132 tons (122 tonnes)?
5. What does the cleaner wrasse clean?
6. Can you name one of the two main residents in the sloth's fur?
7. Which are tougher – mice or rats?
8. What makes frogs light up from the inside?
9. How do crocodiles know their eggs have hatched in their mud nest?
10. What makes luminous jellyfish glow?

Silhouettes

These silhouettes are all of animals or objects that are in Part One. Can you guess which ones they are?

Which part of the world?

Which part or parts of the world…

1. …is pitch-black all the time?
2. …are exposed to air and water twice a day?
3. …is made by animals and stretches for 1,260 miles (2,028km) along the coast?
4. …shields the lynx from Arctic winds?
5. …are scorching by day and freezing at night?
6. …is a frozen ocean?
7. …have the world's biggest plants and trees?
8. …are too hot for farm animals but not for antelopes, zebras, termites and anteaters?
9. …is a whole continent, but inland, only has a few insects living in it?
10. …have plenty of food and shelter, but also much noise and pollution?

Animal actions

All of these sentences describe a particular kind of animal, or animal behavior. Can you match them with one of the words from the list below?

1. An animal which hunts other animals.
2. Keeping an egg warm so it will hatch.
3. Animals which drift in the sea.
4. An animal which feeds milk to its young.
5. How animals change to suit their environment over many thousands of years.
6. Sleeping through winter to avoid the cold.
7. Animals which come out at night.
8. An animal which eats plants.
9. An animal which lives on land but returns to the water to breed.
10. A large group of plant-eating animals.

Evolution Predator Nocturnal Herbivore Amphibian Herd Hibernation Incubation Plankton Mammal

Close-ups

These are all parts of animals that have appeared in Part One. Which animals are they?

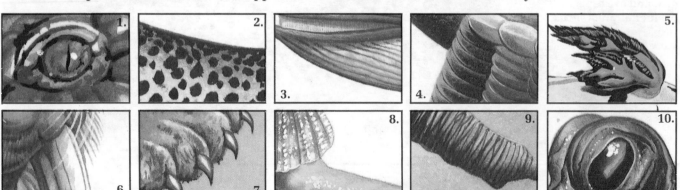

Where in the world?

Can you name these animals and match them with the country, continent or region in which they live?

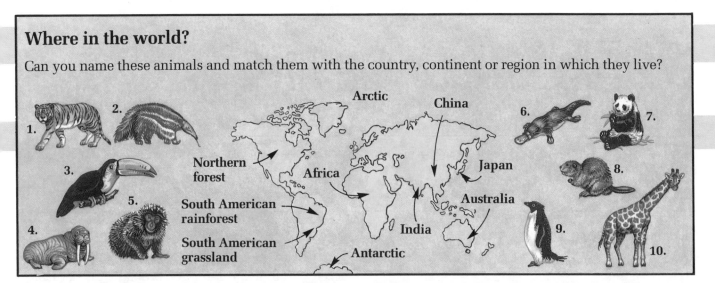

True or false?

1. Lionfish eat zebrafish.
2. Gorillas are vegetarians.
3. Whales cannot breathe underwater.
4. Pigeons have evolved from penguins.
5. Almost three-quarters of the world is covered with water.
6. One in four mammals in the world is a bat.
7. When animals hibernate their blood freezes.
8. Some frogs can fly.
9. The rhino's horn has magical powers.
10. Mudskippers eat mud.

Which animal?

1. Which reptile winds itself along the desert leaving wavy lines in the sand?
2. Which mammal has a tongue half the length of its body?
3. Which insect eats its mate?
4. Which fish sleeps in a bubble of slime?
5. Which mammal's fur grows from its stomach towards its back?
6. Which fish blows itself into a ball if threatened?
7. Which rodents have spread throughout the world on ships?
8. Which bird flies from one end of the world to the other, twice a year?
9. Which insect can eat plastic wiring?
10. Which fish shoots drops of water at insects?

What eats what?

Which of these animals eats the animal or plant in the blue panel below?

Odd one out

1. Which one of these has only one or two babies at a time: rabbit, whale, rat?
2. Which one of these is not a nighttime animal: moth, tapir, owl, butterfly?
3. Which one of these is plankton: anglerfish, walrus, jellyfish, lobster?
4. Which one of these cannot survive out of water: mudskipper, crab, anemone, sole?
5. Which one of these northern forest animals does not hibernate: woodchuck, lynx, lemming.
6. Which one of these seashore creatures does not burrow under the sand: cockle, crab, razorshell, barnacle?
7. Which one of these only lives in the Arctic: seal, walrus, Arctic tern?
8. Which one of these animals is not a herd or pack animal: wolf, lion, gorilla, leopard?
9. Which one of these is not a fish: lionfish, butterflyfish, silverfish, pufferfish?
10. Which one of these is a fast mover: army ant, sloth, anemone, tuna?

Quiz answers

The answers to the 12 quizzes from *The animal world* to *Extraordinary animals* are on the next four pages. Give yourself one point for every answer that you get right.

The chart below helps you find out how well you have done in each quiz.

0-5	Read through the answers, then try the quiz again. See how many answers you can remember this time.
6-10	Quite good. Think more carefully about the questions and you might get more answers right.
11-14	Good score. If you get this score on most of the quizzes, you have done very well.
15	Excellent. If you do this well in more than half the quizzes, you are an animal expert!

Your score overall

You can find out your average score over all 12 quizzes like this:

1. Add up your scores on all 12 quizzes.
2. Divide this total by 12. This is your average score. How well did you do?

General knowledge

All the answers to general knowledge questions are marked ★. These questions are probably the hardest in the quizzes. Add up how many of them you got right across all 12 quizzes. There are 40 of them in total. If you got over 25 right, your general knowledge is good.

The animal world

★ 1. Snakes are reptiles.
★ 2. Humans are mammals.
★ 3. The ostrich cannot fly.
★ 4. b) The zebra is only found in Africa.

Zebra   **Africa**

★ 5. The kangaroo carries its young in a pouch. Baby kangaroos are called joeys.
6. b) Dogs are found all over the world.
7. True. The whale is a mammal.
★ 8. Nine. The seal, lobster, shrimp, crab, octopus, seashell, ray, cod and grouper live in the sea. (Crocodiles are found by river banks and swamps.)
9. c) The salmon is a fish.
10. a) Charles Darwin. He suggested the theory of evolution in his book *On the origin of species* published in 1859.
11. c) The iguana is not an insect. It is a reptile.
12. Lions are carnivores.
13. a) When a whole species of animal dies out, this is called extinction.

The dodo became extinct by 1800.

14. True. The Ancient Egyptians worshipped a cat goddess called Bast.
15. The right order for this food chain is cabbage, caterpillar, thrush, fox.

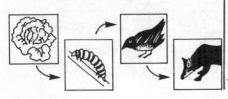

Animal families

1. The correct order is: b) sperm whale; a) elephant; c) giant clam.

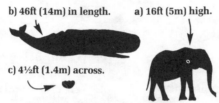

b) 46ft (14m) in length.   **a) 16ft (5m) high.**

c) 4½ft (1.4m) across.

2. c) Warming an egg to hatch it is called incubation.
★ 3. Penguins eat fish.
4. False. Penguins cannot fly at all, though they are very good swimmers.
★ 5. Ducks' eggs are bigger than hens' eggs.
6. d) A rocket fish is not a real fish.
7. b) Beating the chest is intended to drive away enemies. Gorillas are really quite gentle, and will rarely attack.
8. Gorillas are herbivores. They eat food such as celery, sugar cane, nettles and thistles.
★ 9. Cuckoos lay their eggs in other birds' nests – leaving them with the task of guarding and feeding their chicks.
★ 10. The kangaroo is only found in Australia, as is the koala bear, emu and duck-billed platypus.

Koala   **Emu**

11. b) Crocodile eggs are covered in mud to keep them warm. Mud keeps heat in like a blanket.
12. False. As far as anyone knows, crocodiles cannot be taught to waltz.
13. True. Baby scorpions will eat each other if there is no other food around.
14. a) Honeybees perform a complex dance to tell other bees in their group where to find food.
★ 15. The cells are made of wax.

Staying alive

1. True. This helps tigers to stalk their prey. They can only run fast over short distances so they need to surprise their prey to catch it.
2. a) Tigers like to eat wild pig.
3. Leopards usually hide their prey in a tree where other carnivores cannot reach it.
4. c) A poodle. The wolf is the largest member of the dog family.

Poodle   **Wolf**

5. b) Lions hunt in packs.
6. b) Moray eels can grow to be 10ft (3m) long.
7. Angler fish use this lure for bait. It entices other fish, who think the lure is food, within range. Score a point if you got the general idea.
8. True. Most webs only last about a day. They are made of silk, which the spider can eat and use again.
9. True. The chameleon can change its color to match its environment.
10. True. The sole can match the squares within three or four minutes.
11. True. The sting is shaped like a hook and buries itself into the bee's victim. The bee tears open its tail when it flies off. Although it dies, its action may have saved other bees.
12. b) Many lizards can shed their tails if they are grabbed by them.
★ 13. Baby spotted deer are called fawns.
★ 14. c) The South American llama is not a deer. It is a relative of the camel.

Llama   **Camel**

★ 15. Caterpillars turn into butterflies or moths. Score a point if you got either or both answers.

Northern forest animals

1. The northern forests cover land in the continents of Europe, Asia, and North America.
2. Humans have hunted the lynx for its fur.
3. The pine marten is named after the pine tree, which is common in the northern forests.

Pine trees

4. True. The moose is the biggest member of the deer family.

Southern pudu. The smallest member of the deer family.

Moose

5. d) The tree tops are too cold and too exposed to danger to offer a good place to hibernate.
6. b) The thrush migrates. All the other animals live in one part of the world all year round.
7. a) The lemming's greatest enemy is the owl.
8. c) You would find beavers in Canada.

Beaver

Canada   USA

9. True. Both beaver parents build small canals to help ferry logs to build their dams.
10. The lodge is made of the same material as the dam – wood, grass and mud.
11. The underwater entrance makes the lodge especially safe. Any creature wanting to get in would have to be able to swim and dive underwater.
12. False. The bears of the northern forests hibernate in winter.
13. b) These bears are grizzly bears.
14. a) The Moscow State Circus trained two teams of bears to play ice hockey (complete with skates and sticks).

15. True. In the wild, bears also eat fish, small mammals and fruit.

Rainforest animals

1. There are no rainforests in Europe. It is too cold for rainforests.
2. True. The harpy eagle is strong enough to carry off a monkey. It can also carry off a sloth.

Harpy eagle

3. False. As far as we know, sloths do not snore.
4. b) Sloths sleep for 15 to 18 hours a day.
5. c) Jaguars are too heavy for thinner branches. They are clever hunters though and can stalk their prey on the ground and even in water.
6. True. The capybara is the largest rodent in the world.

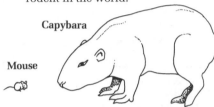

Capybara

Mouse

7. False. The tapir is a plant eater. It comes out at night because there are fewer animals around that might catch and eat it.
★ 8. Parrots eat fruit and seeds. Score one point for either or both answers.
9. d) The condor is not a parrot. It is a type of South American vulture. There are 315 different types of parrot in the world.

Condor

★ 10. The marmoset is a monkey, like the howler and spider monkey.
11. True. A marmoset is about the size of a kitten. It is the smallest monkey in the world.

Marmoset   Kitten

12. No. If it has to, a sloth can move at 0.6mph (1km/h), considerably faster than army ants.
13. Yes, rainforests do have people living in them. Pygmies and Amazonian Indians are rainforest dwellers.
14. c) Howler monkeys can be heard 10 miles (16km) away.
15. b) The tapir makes the least noise, to avoid being heard by hunting jaguars.

City wildlife *and* The night shift

★ 1. In the legend, the Pied Piper drove rats out of the German town of Hamelin. When the town council did not pay him his agreed fee, he took all the town's children and they were never seen again!
2. b) The tile termite is not a real insect.
3. c) A fly usually lives for 10 weeks.
4. False. Mice and rats are both rodents, but they are not the same species.
5. b) A female rat can have 12 babies every eight weeks.
★ 6. Pigeons are seen most in any city. They do not need to hide themselves because they live in places that are difficult to reach.

Pigeon

7. Two. Crocodiles are too big to find shelter, and too dangerous to live close by humans. Score a point if you got either of these answers.
8. True. Owls' eyes are too large to move in their heads. They make up for this by being able to turn their heads around almost half a circle.

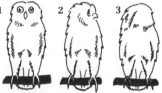

1   2   3

★ 9. Yes, vampire bats do exist. They prefer cattle blood to human blood though.

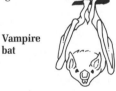

Vampire bat

10. False. Bats cannot pick up radio signals.
11. b) Glowworms glow to attract a mate.
12. c) The eagle is not a nighttime animal.
13. b) The potto is a type of loris. Lorises are forest-dwelling mammals, similar to monkeys.
★ 14. Moles make their homes in the ground. They are small, burrowing mammals which eat worms and insects.

Entrance to burrow

Mole

15. True. The light of several fireflies is just bright enough to read by.

The open ocean

1. The most fertile areas of the sea are all off the coast. Score a point if you got the general idea. Shallow seas usually have the most life, and water is always shallow by the coast.

★ 2. The Pacific is the biggest ocean in the world. It contains 52% of the world's sea water.

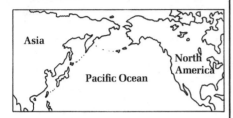

★ 3. Large groups of fish are called shoals or schools. Score a point for either.
4. b) Fish sleep in a trance. They have no eyelids so their eyes stay open when they sleep.
5. c) The prawn is a crustacean.

Prawn

6. False. No birds have gills.
7. d) The parrot is not a good swimmer. Parrots live in trees in rainforests.
★ 8. Whale leaping is called breaching.
9. b) Whales often have barnacles living on them. These are usually found on the head, flippers and tail.

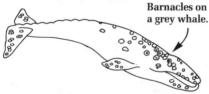

Barnacles on a grey whale.

★ 10. Whales usually have one or two calves. These calves are born at sea. Some sea mammals, like seals and walruses, have their calves on land.
11. True. Plankton are so tiny that 200,000 could live in 1.3 cubic yards (a cubic meter) of sea water.
★ 12. Herring are not plankton. They can swim independently of the ocean tides and currents.
13. a) The word plankton comes from the Greek word *planktos*, which means wanderer.
14. a) This fish is called a viper fish. It is about 1ft (30cm) long.

The hatchet fish is another type of deep sea fish.

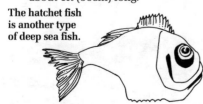

15. False. The light comes from pouches of luminous bacteria on the side of the fish.

Life at the edge of the sea

1. These sea birds have long legs so they can wade in the shallow water at the edge of the beach.
2. a) These patterns are made by burrowing worms.
3. a) Tides are caused by the moon and the sun.
4. False. However, razor shells are called this because they look like old-fashioned razors. This shape helps them move up and down quickly in their burrows.

Old-fashioned razor

★ 5. People eat crabs, oysters and cockles. Score a point if you got two or more of these.
6. a) The digging muscle is called a foot.
7. b) Barnacles settle on ships. In fact they settle on most things in the sea, from driftwood to discarded shoes.
8. c) You would not find a salamander in a rock pool. Salamanders are amphibians which usually live in mountains and caves.
9. There are no coral reefs in Europe. The water is too cold for coral.
★ 10. The Great Barrier Reef is off the coast of Australia.
11. The coral animal looks rather like the sea anemone. They both come from a class of animals called coelenterates (pronounced sel-ent-erates). Their bodies are very similar in structure.

Coral   Anemone

12. b) The parrotfish takes its name from its hard, parrot-like beak. The coral that it crushes makes sand for the nearest beach.

Parrot fish

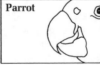

Parrot

13. The sea urchin has spikes like sharp knitting needles, to protect it from being eaten. Some fish can bite off the spikes though, leaving it defenseless.
14. False. Sponges are not used to make sponge cake.
15. True. Stonefish have poisonous spines on their backs which can be fatal to any diver that steps on them.

Poisonous spines

Stonefish

Living without water *and* Living at the ends of the earth

1. d) Kenya is not a desert. It is a country in eastern Africa.

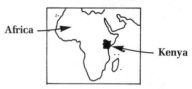

Africa   Kenya

2. Europe is the only continent which does not have a desert.
3. b) The camel's hump stores fat.
4. c) Camels with one hump are called dromedaries. Camels with two humps are called bactrians. You can remember which is which if you think of a D for Dromedary as having one "hump", and a B for Bactrian as having two "humps".

Dromedary

Bactrian

5. True. Camels can drink up to 35gal (136l) in a single day when they get the chance.
★ 6. Fertile areas of the desert are called oases.
7. True. Vegetation can provide all of the addax's water requirements.
8. b) The cactus is a desert plant.
9. The central point of the Arctic is known as the North Pole.
★ 10. Score a point if you got one or more of these: black bear, brown bear, grizzly bear, Himalayan bear, Kodiak bear, sun bear.
11. No, Africa is over twice the size of the Antarctic.

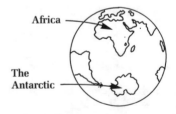

Africa

The Antarctic

12. True. The Antarctic is almost entirely covered in ice. In some parts this ice is over 2 miles (3km) thick.
13. a) Seals are mammals, like whales and walruses.
14. c) The flamingo can fly.

Flamingo

15. Polar bears probably would eat penguins if they lived in the same part of the world. Fortunately for the penguins who live in the Antarctic, polar bears only live in the Arctic.

Grassland wildlife.

1. c) The rhino uses its horn to attack its enemies.

The horn can grow to 5ft (1.58m).

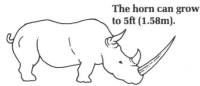

2. a) The horn is made from keratin.
3. Animals that eat other animals are called carnivores (from the Latin *carnis* – flesh, *vorare* – to devour).
4. There are four. The rhino, elephant, zebra and wildebeest are all plant-eaters.
5. b) The stripes are for camouflage. They are especially good at disguising the zebra's shape from a distance.
6. True. Newborn zebras are in great danger from predators. Walking with the herd protects them.
7. When animals travel long distances this is called migration. Zebras and antelopes also migrate across the grassland in search of food.
8. This is true, but it only happened in zoos, when the two animals were kept together. In the wild, these two animals live in different parts of the world.

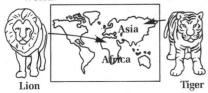

Lion   Asia   Africa   Tiger

9. c) Termite mounds are made of mud. Termites make the mounds by chewing earth and forming it into mud bricks.
10. False. The lion lives in Africa, and the giant anteater lives in South America.
11. a) The anteater's bushy tail helps it keep warm. It curls its tail around itself when it is cold.
12. No. The giraffe is the tallest animal in the world: Some giraffes grow as tall as 20ft (6.1m).

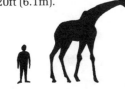

13. Termites live in a termitarium.
14. d) An elephant does not use its trunk to whistle, though it can make a loud trumpeting noise with it.
15. True. Elephants, rhinos and hippos cover themselves in mud to keep clean. When the mud dries it falls off, taking with it irritating ticks and fleas.

Elephant

Animal oddities

★ 1. All three of these spiders have poison powerful enough to make people ill. Score a point if you guessed they were poisonous.

Black widow spider

2. True. Jumping spiders can jump impressive distances. When they stalk their prey their eyes turn from green to brown.
3. c) Insects copy all these shapes, except the red berry. Red berries are eaten by birds and are very conspicuous.
★ 4. Anemones, corals and jellyfish all have stinging tentacles.
5. c) The raspberry jellyfish is not a real jellyfish. There is one called a sea wasp though, and another called a sea gooseberry.
★ 6. The giant anteater also has a sticky tongue and eats ants and termites.
★ 7. From the biggest to the smallest, the right order is pangolin, platypus, mudskipper, jumping spider.

Pangolin 36in (90cm).
Platypus 27in (70cm).

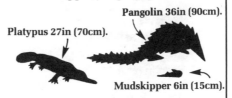

Mudskipper 6in (15cm).
Jumping spider ½in (1.25cm).

8. False. (Pacific islanders use a shell called a conch as a trumpet though.)
9. d) Elephant tusks are made of ivory. Everything else on the list is made of keratin.
10. The nudibranch is similar to a slug.

Slug
Nudibranch

11. False. Platypus babies have no special name. There are usually one or two of them in a litter.
12. False. Birds are too big, both to be knocked off, and eaten.
13. Archer fish live in rivers. There are very few insects in oceans.
14. a) The air tank divers use is called an aqualung.

Aqualung

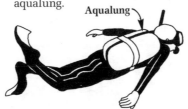

15. b) Male mudskippers attract females by waving their back fins.

Extraordinary animals

1. False. Of 250 types of shark, only 20 are known to eat humans. Most will swim away if they see a human.
2. b) A shark's skin is covered with barbed scales. These cut or bruise any animal that brushes against the shark.
3. a) Mayflies only live for a day as adults. They hatch, lay eggs and die.
4. c) It is thought that whales sing to let other whales know where to find them.
★ 5. Blue whales eat plankton. They have huge brush-like bristles in their mouths, called baleen. These filter the minute plankton out of the water.

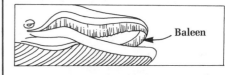

Baleen

6. a) Mosquitoes are eaten by spiders.
★ 7. You may find a sponge in your bathroom. Most bathroom sponges are likely to be artificial ones though.

Artificial sponge   **Natural sponge**

8. True. Arctic and Antarctic summers have very long days and very short nights. Some terns have lived to be over thirty, and have probably flown a distance similar to the moon and back —over 500,000 miles (800,000km).
9. a) The Arctic tern eats crustaceans.
10. True. Young swifts spend the first two years of their life in the air.
★ 11. Swifts eat insects.
12. The crescent shape. This is ideal for pushing an animal smoothly through air or water.

Swift
Crescent shape
Sailfish

13. True. Cheetahs were used to hunt antelope. They wore hoods until they were unleashed, like trained falcons do today.
★ 14. From largest to smallest the correct order is: lion, cheetah, lynx, domestic cat.

Lion 11ft (3.5m).
Cheetah 6½ft (1.75m).
Lynx 3½ft (1m).
Domestic cat 2½ft (0.75m).

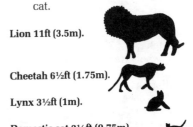

15. a) The snail is the slowest. Garden snails move at 0.03mph (0.05km/h).

Animal Megaquiz answers

There are 100 points in the whole of the Animal Megaquiz. Score a point for each correct answer. If you score over 50 you have done well. Over 75 is excellent. You can find out more about each answer on the page listed after it in brackets.

What do you know?

1. The sea (page 14).
2. a) shark (page 14).
3. c) cormorant (page 14).
4. Blue whale (page 25).
5. Other fish (page 17).
6. Algae, or moths (page 10).
7. Rats (page 12).
8. The glowworms they have eaten (page 13).
9. The babies squeak (page 5).
10. Luminious bacteria (page 22).

Silhouettes

1. Jellyfish (page 22).
2. Scorpion (page 5).
3. Pufferfish (page 17).
4. Termite (page 21).
5. Flying squirrel (page 11).
6. Shark (page 24).
7. Termite mound (page 21).
8. Rhinoceros (page 20).
9. Turtle (page 14).
10. Bat (page 13).

Which part of the world?

1. The depths of the ocean (page 15).
2. The seashore (page 16).
3. Great Barrier Reef (page 17).
4. The northern forests (page 8).
5. The desert (page 18).
6. The Arctic (page 19).
7. Tropical rainforest (page 10).
8. Grasslands (page 20).
9. Antarctica (page 19).
10. Cities (page 12).

Animal actions

1. Predator (page 6).
2. Incubation (page 4).
3. Plankton (page 15).
4. Mammal (page 2).
5. Evolution (page 3).
6. Hibernation (page 8).
7. Nocturnal (page 13).
8. Herbivore (page 3).
9. Amphibian (page 2).
10. Herd (page 20).

Close-ups

1. Crocodile (page 5).
2. Cheetah (page 25).
3. Blue whale (page 25).
4. Spine-tailed swift (page 24).
5. Nudibranch (page 23).
6. Walrus (page 19).
7. Tiger (page 6).
8. Cockle (page 16).
9. Elephant (page 21).
10. Mudskipper (page 23).

Where in the world?

1. Tiger/India (page 6).
2. Giant anteater/South American grassland (page 21).
3. Toucan/South American rainforest (page 22).
4. Walrus/Arctic (page 19).
5. Macaque monkey/Japan (page 9).
6. Platypus/Australia (page 23).
7. Panda/China (page 12).
8. Beaver/Northern forests (page 9).
9. Penguin/Antarctic (page 19).
10. Giraffe/Africa (page 21).

True or false?

1. False.
2. True (page 4).
3. True (page 14).
4. False.
5. True (page 14).
6. True (page 13).
7. False.
8. True (page 11).
9. False.
10. False.

Which animal?

1. Sidewinder snake (page 18).
2. Pangolin (page 22).
3. Praying mantis (page 5).
4. Parrotfish (page 17).
5. Sloth (page 10).
6. Pufferfish (page 17).
7. *Either* rats *or* mice (page 12).
8. *Either* tern *or* Arctic tern (page 24).
9. Termite (page 12).
10. Archerfish (page 22).

What eats what?

1. (j) Seal (page 19).
2. (d) Zebra (page 20).
3. (i) Greenfly (page 3).
4. (f) Grass (page 20).
5. (h) Tapir (page 8).
6. (b) Mouse (page 13).
7. (a) Coral (page 17).
8. (e) Salmon (page 9).
9. (g) Monkey (page 10).
10. (c) Leaves (page 2) .

Odd one out

1. Whale (page 4).
2. Butterfly (page 13).
3. Jellyfish (page 15).
4. Sole (page 7).
5. Lynx (page 8).
6. Barnacle (page 16).
7. Walrus (page 19).
8. Leopard (page 6).
9. Silverfish (page 12).
10. Tuna (page 24).

Part Two

USBORNE FACTS & FUN ABOUT SCIENCE

Paul Dowswell and Marit Claridge

Edited by Judy Tatchell and Lisa Miles

Designed by Ruth Russell and Fiona Brown

Illustrated by Chris Lyon and Chris Shields

Additional text by Carol Varley

Consultants: Peter McKerchar, Geoffrey Puplett, John and Margaret Rostron

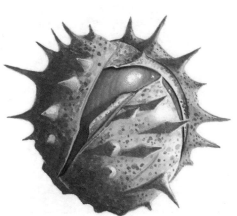

Contents

About Part Two

Part Two of the book is an introduction to scientific ideas. It looks at what things are made of and how they work — from plants and animals, to racing cars and video cameras. It also explains natural forces and effects, such as gravity, electricity, sound and light.

How to do the quizzes

Throughout the book there are quiz questions to answer as you go along, printed in italic type, *like this*. Some of the questions rely on your general knowledge, others have clues elsewhere on the page. Keep a note of your answers and check them against the answers on pages 60–63.

The Science Megaquiz

On pages 58–59 is the Science Megaquiz — a set of ten quick quizzes to test you on your general knowledge and what you have read about in Part Two.

Exploring space

The whole of space and everything in it is known as the universe. Scientists do not know how large the universe is, but the part they do know about contains millions of groups of stars, called galaxies. Each galaxy is in turn made up of millions of stars.

Where is the Earth?

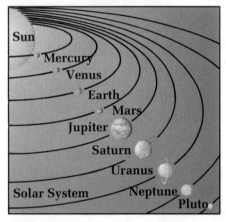

Sun
Mercury
Venus
Earth
Mars
Jupiter
Saturn
Uranus
Solar System
Neptune
Pluto

The Earth is one of nine planets which circle around a central star, the Sun. The Sun and its planets are called a solar system. The Sun is a star in the galaxy called the Milky Way.

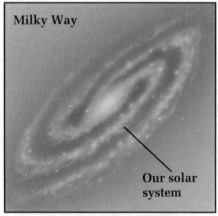

Milky Way

Our solar system

As far as we know, the Earth is the only planet that provides the air, water and warmth that living things need. It is just the right distance away from the Sun for water to exist as a liquid, rather than gas or ice. Earth's atmosphere also protects it from getting too hot or too cold.

1. Venus, Neptune and Mars are named after: a) Roman gods; b) astronomers; c) Egyptian pharaohs.

2. Are Sirius, Betelgeuse and Alpha Centauri stars or planets?

How old is the universe?

Most scientists believe that the universe began about 15 thousand million years ago. An enormous explosion, called the Big Bang, created an immensely hot, dense fireball. Everything in the universe came from this fireball. The force of this explosion was so great that stars and galaxies are still being blasted away from one another, and the universe is still expanding.

The fireball was made of hydrogen gas.

The gas formed a dense cloud of particles which broke into separate clouds.

These clouds became galaxies of stars, like our own Milky Way.

How do we know what is in space?

Scientists use a variety of telescopes to see what is out in space. For example, optical telescopes use lenses to magnify light. These telescopes were first used about 400 years ago and enabled astronomers to get a closer look at the night sky. Today, photographic film and electronic sensors can record faint images that the eye cannot see.

Stars and planets give off other rays besides the light we can see. Telescopes can now detect radio waves, ultra-violet and X-ray signals from stars which are so distant they cannot be seen by even the most powerful optical telescopes.

3. Radio waves from stars contain: a) blips, bleeps and hisses; b) alien traffic reports; c) light music.

4. Einstein was the first scientist to use a telescope. True or false?

Why is the Sun hot?

The Sun is an immense ball of burning hydrogen gas. It releases huge amounts of energy in a similar way to a nuclear bomb, in the form of heat and light. The Sun is so big it is taking millions of years to burn.

The temperature at the surface is about 11,000°F (6,000°C).

Sun

The middle of the Sun is 2,500 times hotter than the surface.

7. One day the Sun will go out. True or false?

8. Is it safe to look directly at the Sun?

9. Which one of these would you find in space: a) a purple pixie; b) a white dwarf; c) a green gremlin?

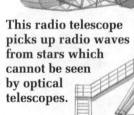

This radio telescope picks up radio waves from stars which cannot be seen by optical telescopes.

5. You can see X-rays and ultra-violet rays. True or false?

6. A group of stars is called: a) a compound; b) a collection; c) a constellation.

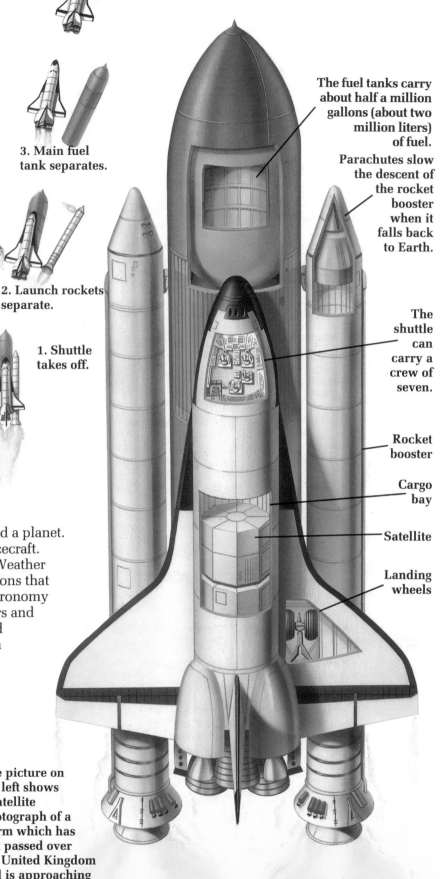

How does a rocket fly?

Rockets need an immense amount of energy to blast themselves out of the Earth's atmosphere. They burn fuel, which creates hot gas which escapes through exhaust nozzles. This produces a force like air rushing out of the end of a balloon, which pushes the rocket forwards.

The space shuttle uses two sets of rockets to blast it into space. Once in space, launch rockets and the main fuel tank fall back to Earth.

The shuttle can launch satellites in space, or carry out scientific experiments. It glides back to Earth and lands like an aircraft.

10. The first spacecraft to land men on the Moon was called: a) Sputnik; b) Apollo 11; c) Starship Enterprise.

11. Dogs have been up in space. True or false?

3. Main fuel tank separates.

2. Launch rockets separate.

1. Shuttle takes off.

The fuel tanks carry about half a million gallons (about two million liters) of fuel.

Parachutes slow the descent of the rocket booster when it falls back to Earth.

The shuttle can carry a crew of seven.

Rocket booster

Cargo bay

Satellite

Landing wheels

What is a satellite?

A satellite is anything that orbits around a planet. The moon is a satellite, and so is a spacecraft. Man-made satellites have many uses. Weather satellites take pictures of cloud formations that can be used to predict the weather. Astronomy satellites send back information on stars and planets. Communication satellites send telephone conversations and television transmissions around the world.

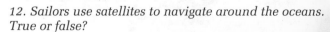

The picture on the left shows a satellite photograph of a storm which has just passed over the United Kingdom and is approaching Scandinavia.

12. Sailors use satellites to navigate around the oceans. True or false?

13. The word "satellite" comes from a Latin word for: a) attendant; b) star; c) spacecraft.

14. Which country was the first to launch a satellite?

15. Yuri Gagarin was the first man: a) on the moon; b) to go into space; c) to drive his spaceship into a satellite.

Did you know?

When astronomers look at stars, they are seeing many of them as they were thousands or millions of years ago. Some of these stars may even no longer exist. Starlight takes this long to reach Earth because distances in space are so huge.

What are things made of ?

Everything in the world, from mountains and oceans, to air and animals, is made of chemicals.

What are chemicals?

All chemicals are made up of minute particles called atoms. The simplest chemicals are made of only one kind of atom and are called elements. Chemicals made up of two or more elements are called compounds. There are around one hundred elements, and over ten million compounds. New compounds are being discovered all the time.

Glass is a compound made of the elements silicon, sodium and oxygen.

Water is a compound made of the elements hydrogen and oxygen.

Copper, which is used in electrical wiring, is an element.

The mercury in a thermometer is an element.

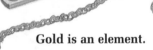

Gold is an element.

Helium is an element. It makes balloons float up in the air.

Sand is a compound made of the elements silicon and oxygen.

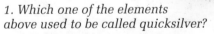

1. Which one of the elements above used to be called quicksilver?

Although food, wood and plastic are very different, most contain the same three elements: hydrogen, carbon and oxygen. What makes them different is the way their atoms have joined together to form larger particles, called molecules, and how these molecules have arranged themselves.

2. Diamonds and coal are both made from the same element. True or false?

3. Which of these is sand not used for: a) making glass; b) putting out fires; c) seasoning food?

What makes something a solid, a liquid or a gas?

Atoms and the molecules they form are always moving, even in things that look still. Whether something is a solid, liquid or gas depends on how much these molecules are moving.

When water is solid ice, the water molecules are packed together evenly. These molecules are moving, but they are only vibrating.

Ice

When water is liquid, the molecules are close together, but are able to slip past each other. Liquids flow because the molecules can move around and change places with each other.

Water

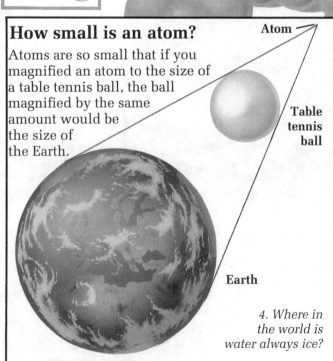

How small is an atom?

Atoms are so small that if you magnified an atom to the size of a table tennis ball, the ball magnified by the same amount would be the size of the Earth.

Atom

Table tennis ball

Earth

4. Where in the world is water always ice?

When water is a gas, steam, the molecules are far apart and moving quickly.

Steam

5. Ice always forms as a cube. True or false?

6. Can iron be turned into a liquid?

*7. Gas squashed into a smaller space is called:
a) commendable; b) contaminated; c) compressed.*

Did you know?

Ancient Greeks guessed that everything was made of atoms two and a half thousand years ago. The word "atom" comes from the Greek word *atomos*, which means "uncuttable."

Is anything smaller than an atom?

Atoms are made of even smaller particles called protons, neutrons and electrons.

Protons and neutrons are found in the middle, or nucleus, of an atom.

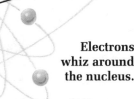

— Nucleus

Electrons whiz around the nucleus.

● Proton
● Neutron
● Electron

Elements such as gold and mercury are different from one another because their atoms have a different number of electrons and protons.

8. Electrons carry: a) specks of dust; b) an electrical charge; c) water molecules.

What is nuclear energy?

Nuclear energy (also called atomic energy) is stored in the nucleus in the middle of an atom. This energy can be released in the form of heat, in two ways. Large atoms can be split in two, or small atoms can be joined to other small atoms. Nuclear energy can be used to make electricity and very powerful weapons.

Nuclear power stations produce energy by heating steam which drives turbines to make electricity.

Heat is produced by nuclear energy.

Turbines make electricity here.

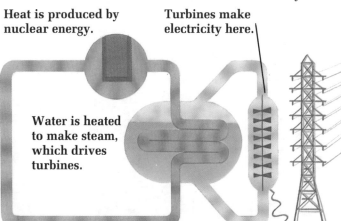

Water is heated to make steam, which drives turbines.

Nuclear bombs produce huge amounts of heat and are tremendously destructive. Some are so powerful that just one could destroy an entire city.

9. Which of these metals is used to make nuclear energy: a) uranium; b) iron; c) copper?

10. Nuclear bombs have only been used against one country. Do you know which one?

Can you see atoms?

It is possible to see atoms with a scanning electron microscope. This can magnify up to around 50 million times by passing a stream of electrons through an object, which then strike a screen. A computer turns the pattern the electrons make into a picture, in which individual atoms are depicted.

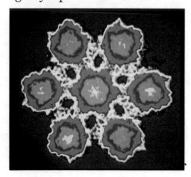

11. A microscope which uses lenses to magnify is called an: a) oracle; b) electrical; c) optical microscope.

12. All nuclear energy is man-made. True or false?

13. Are smells solids, liquids or gases?

14. Which squashed gas do divers, astronauts and firemen carry in tanks, to enable them to breathe?

15. Unravel each of these words to make the names of three elements: dogl, propec, geynox.

Using materials

The earth and sea are full of useful substances which are called raw materials. Raw materials are the basic ingredients for anything that people make.

What are raw materials?

Raw materials are natural materials. Most look different from the products they are used to make. Metals, for example, come from rocks called ores. This diagram shows some raw materials and their products.

1. Can you match these raw materials with their products?

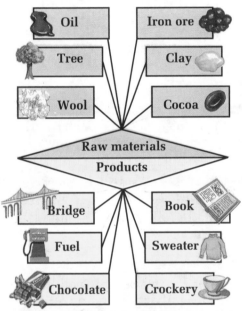

Oil
Iron ore
Tree
Clay
Wool
Cocoa
Raw materials
Products
Bridge
Book
Fuel
Sweater
Chocolate
Crockery

2. Which one of these is a man-made material: a) wool; b) copper; c) nylon?

How are new materials made from raw materials?

Some raw materials, such as wood, can be used as they are. Others, such as metal ores, contain useful chemicals which have to be extracted before they can be used. This can be done with heat, or by combining the raw material with other chemicals.

Ores generally produce only one product: the metal inside them. Oil, called crude oil in its natural state, is more complex. It contains thousands of chemicals which can be turned into millions of products.

How are new materials made from oil?

The thousands of chemicals in oil can be separated, or refined, by a process called fractional distillation. Many of the products of distillation, such as diesel oil, can be used as they are, but many others need further refining. This diagram shows how a distillation tower works.

3. Which area is famous for producing crude oil: a) Texas, USA; b) the North Pole; c) Paris, France?

4. Does cooking oil come from crude oil?

1. Crude oil is heated to a very high temperature, and most of it enters the distillation tower as a gas.

4. The chemicals obtained from crude oil can be used to make many things, such as medicines, detergents, waxes, plastics and fuel.

3. Chemicals in the gas cool to a liquid at different temperatures. They are collected at different levels in the tower.

2. As the gas rises, it cools.

How are materials used?

When designers create a product, they specify the most suitable materials for the job. For example, in motor racing, materials are chosen to keep the driver safe and also to help the car perform well. This picture shows how some of these materials are used in the car and clothing of a top racing driver. Many of the materials come from metal ores and crude oil, but plant and animal materials are also used.

The car body is made of a mixture, or composite, of man-made materials known as plastics. One of these plastics is called Kevlar,* which comes from the chemicals in crude oil. Kevlar gives the car strength. It is a very useful material because not only is it strong and rigid, it is also very light. It has many other uses, such as in the manufacture of bulletproof vests and the bodies of boats and aircraft.

5. Why is it important that the car is light in weight?

Seat

Steering wheel

The seat and steering wheel are covered in suede, a velvety kind of leather. Suede helps the driver grip.

The tires are mainly made of rubber, which grips the track well. Layers of steel and fabric give strength and flexibility.

Rubber
Steel
Fabric

6. What kind of raw material is rubber made from?

*Du Pont's registered trademark

How is metal taken from ores?

There are about 80 known metals. A few, such as gold, exist on their own, but most are found within ores, which are mined.

Metals are extracted from their ore by heating them with other materials. The atoms in these substances are rearranged to make new substances. This process is called a chemical reaction.

The diagram shows how iron is extracted from iron ore by a process called smelting.

10. More than three-quarters of elements are metals. True or false?

11. This type of furnace is called an: a) open; b) closed; c) blast furnace.

12. Some metals explode if they are dropped in water. True or false?

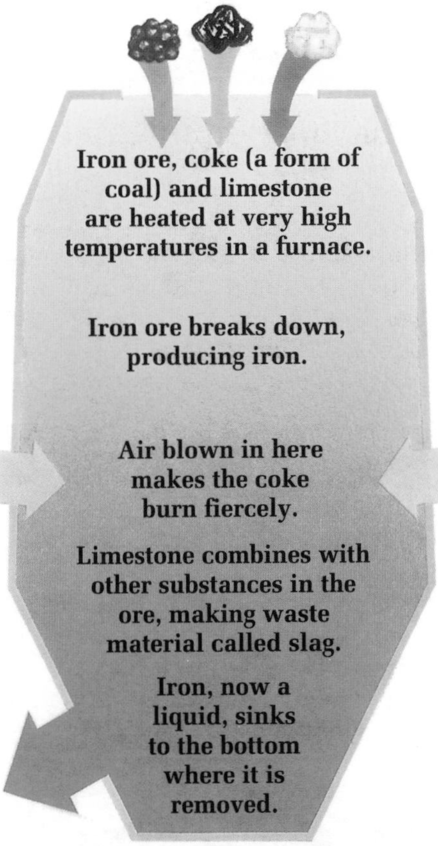

Iron ore, coke (a form of coal) and limestone are heated at very high temperatures in a furnace.
Iron ore breaks down, producing iron.
Air blown in here makes the coke burn fiercely.
Limestone combines with other substances in the ore, making waste material called slag.
Iron, now a liquid, sinks to the bottom where it is removed.

Did you know?

Gold is such a precious metal that scientists, known as alchemists, spent centuries trying to turn cheap metals, such as lead, into gold. They failed, but their work became the basis of our knowledge of metals and alloys today.

13. The purity of gold is measured in: a).lead; b) pearls; c) carats.

14. Alchemists are named after Al the Chemist – the first man to try to turn lead into gold. True or false?

15. A thin sheet of gold is called gold: a) leaf; b) sheaf; c) reef.

Gloves
Visor
Helmet
The suspension springs help the car go over bumps smoothly.

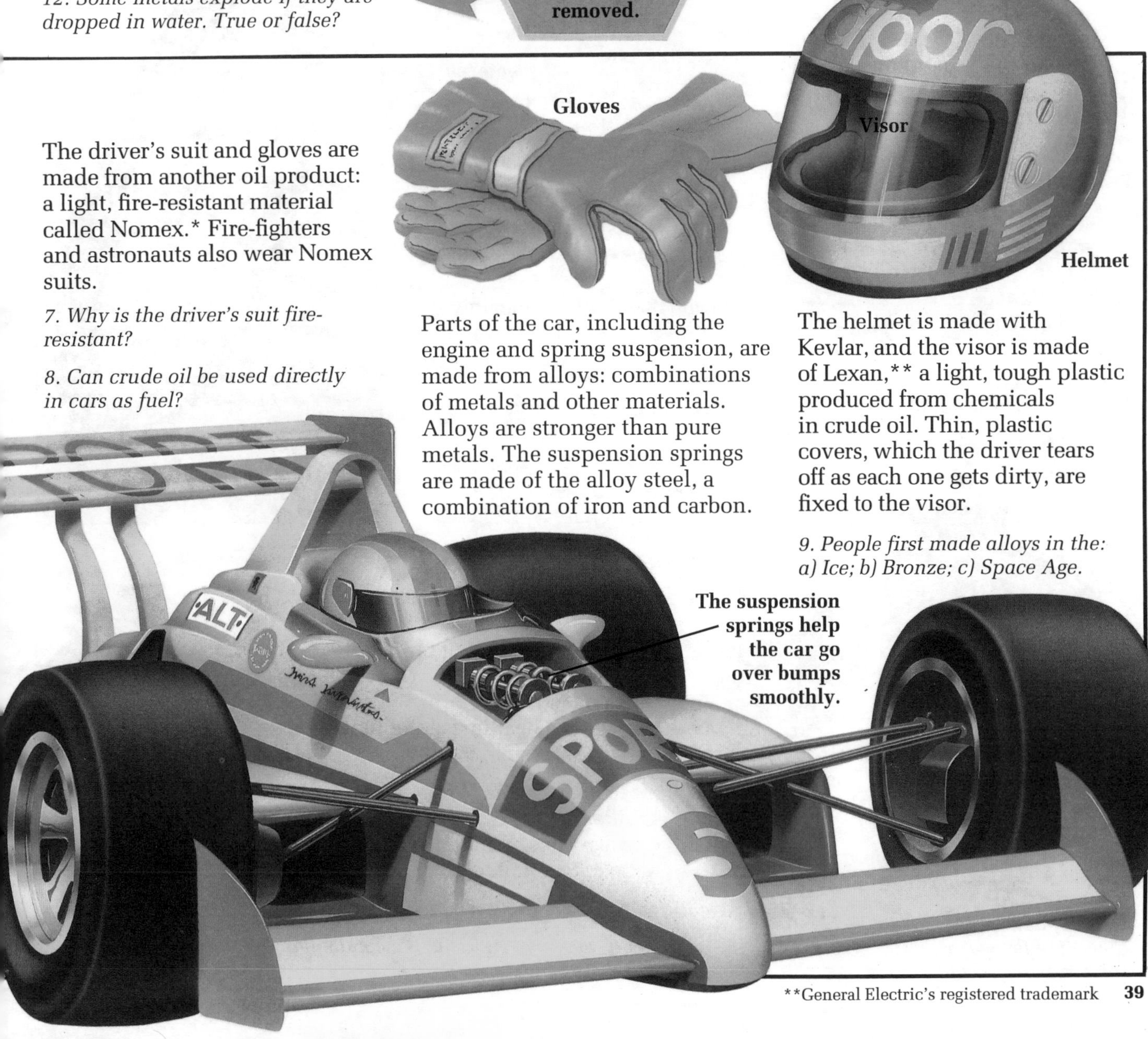

The driver's suit and gloves are made from another oil product: a light, fire-resistant material called Nomex.* Fire-fighters and astronauts also wear Nomex suits.

7. Why is the driver's suit fire-resistant?

8. Can crude oil be used directly in cars as fuel?

Parts of the car, including the engine and spring suspension, are made from alloys: combinations of metals and other materials. Alloys are stronger than pure metals. The suspension springs are made of the alloy steel, a combination of iron and carbon.

The helmet is made with Kevlar, and the visor is made of Lexan,** a light, tough plastic produced from chemicals in crude oil. Thin, plastic covers, which the driver tears off as each one gets dirty, are fixed to the visor.

9. People first made alloys in the: a) Ice; b) Bronze; c) Space Age.

**General Electric's registered trademark

Moving, flying and floating

Deep in space, a moving object will carry on at the same speed, in the same direction endlessly. This does not happen on Earth. Forces act on everything, making them speed up, slow down, change direction and even change shape.

What is a force?

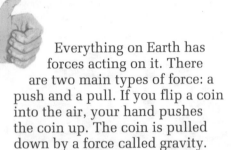

Pull of gravity

Push up

Everything on Earth has forces acting on it. There are two main types of force: a push and a pull. If you flip a coin into the air, your hand pushes the coin up. The coin is pulled down by a force called gravity.

What is gravity?

Gravity pulls all objects towards one another. However, it is a weak force. Only huge objects, such as planets, have a strong enough gravity to pull things to them.

Gravity pulls objects down.

Force of ground pushes up.

Gravity pulls everything towards the middle of the Earth. Things are not sucked in because the ground pushes up against them. Gravity, like all forces, has an opposite force working against it.

1. Astronauts on the way to the Moon go most of the way with their rocket engines switched off. True or false?

40

What makes things heavy or light?

How heavy something is depends on how big it is, how heavy its atoms are, and how closely these atoms are packed together. A steel ball weighs more than an apple of the same size because its atoms are heavier: it is said to have a greater density. It feels heavier because gravity pulls harder on denser materials.

2. Is stone more dense than chocolate?

3. Steel is made from copper and lead. True or false?

Apple

Steel ball

How do forces work?

This picture shows how forces act on a bike when you are riding along. The different forces affect how the bike moves and how fast it is able to go.

1. The force of the Earth's gravity pulls the bike down against the road.

2. The ground pushes in the opposite direction against the wheels of the bike.

3. As you turn the pedals, the wheels are pushed around. The wheels push the bike forwards.

4. Air pushes in the opposite direction to your body and the bike, as you ride along.

4. In a race, why do cyclists crouch down low over the handlebars?

5. Which type of bike is made for two riders: a) a tandem; b) a unicycle; c) a tricycle?

What makes things slow down?

Objects pushing against each other, such as a wheel pushing against the ground, create a force called friction. Friction slows moving objects down. It also produces heat. This is why bike wheels feel hot when you have been riding. Some of the bike's energy is turned into heat instead of moving the wheels, which slows the bike down.

Brakes work using friction. When you work the brakes on a bike, the brake blocks are pulled against the wheel rims. Friction acts between them, bringing the bike to a halt.

6. Would you feel more friction on ice or on gravel?

7. You can get a friction burn from: a) a candle flame; b) boiling water; c) sliding down a rope.

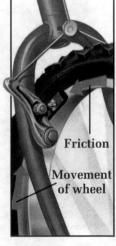

Friction

Movement of wheel

How do planes fly?

Planes need tremendous power to lift them into the air. Their engines give them the power to accelerate forwards, while the shape of their body and wings helps them to lift upwards.

Gravity pulls everything downwards. However, planes stay in the sky because of the way that air pushes on them. Air presses on objects from all sides, and slow-moving air pushes harder than fast-moving air.

Planes' wings are shaped to make the air under the wings travel slower than the air going over the wings. When a plane reaches a certain speed, the slower air beneath the wings pushes harder than the air going over them, forcing the plane into the sky. This force is called lift.

8. Most birds have hollow bones. True or false?

9. The first people to fly used aircraft which were driven by: a) paddles; b) propellers; c) rockets.

10. Do all aircraft have wings?

11. Some aircraft can fly without engines. True or false?

The engines push the plane forwards.

Air flow

The top of the wing is curved, so air flowing over it travels farther and faster, to catch up with the air flowing underneath.

Cross-section of wing

Air going under the wing travels less distance than air going over it, so it travels more slowly.

Push down

Faster-moving air pushes down with less force.

Cross-section of wing

Push up

Slower-moving air pushes up with more force.

How does a ship float?

Some materials, such as polystyrene and paper, float because they are less dense than water. Other materials, such as metal, sink because they are more dense than water. The force of gravity pulling on them is greater than the force of water pushing up against them.

Even so, steel ships with heavy loads can float. There are two reasons why. Ships' bodies, or hulls, push a lot of water down beneath them. This is called displacement. The water then pushes back up against the ship, holding it up. This upward force of the water is called upthrust.

The ship and cargo push down.

The water pushes up.

12. Would an empty ship sit higher or lower in the sea?

13. Does cork sink or float in water?

14. A submarine sinks by: a) rolling over; b) pointing its nose down; c) filling tanks with water.

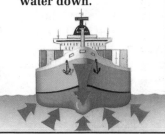

The hull is wide, so that it pushes a lot of water down.

Also, ships are not solid. They have air spaces inside them, such as storage holds. Air makes the ship less dense, so that it pushes down with less force. If the force of the ship pushing down is equal to the upthrust of the water, the ship will float.

Did you know?

Over 300 years ago, in the 1660s, the scientist Isaac Newton was the first person to realize how gravity worked. One story says that the idea first came to him when he saw an apple fall from a tree and hit the ground.

15. Isaac Newton was also well known for:
a) painting portraits; b) studying mathematics;
c) writing romantic novels.

Making things work

In order for something to grow, move, light up, or do any sort of work at all, it needs energy. Without energy, there would be no life.

What is energy?

There are many different forms of energy. Some are shown below. Energy does not always stay in the same form, but can change from one form, such as chemical energy, to another, such as heat energy.

Heat energy

Something hot has more energy than something cold because its atoms are moving around faster. Heat energy can spread from one place to another.

Light energy

Light is a form of energy that moves very fast, in straight lines. Nothing travels faster than light. It is usually given out by things that are very hot.

The hot filament of a light bulb gives out light energy.

Chemical energy

Energy can be stored in the form of chemicals. Animals and plants contain chemical energy in the form of food. Our main fuels, coal, oil and natural gas, are also stores of chemical energy.

Sound energy

Sound energy travels in waves, called sound waves. Sound waves move through the air, making it vibrate. When the sound waves reach your ears you hear them as sounds.

Potential energy

Potential energy is the stored energy an object has because of its position. A spring that is squeezed or stretched has potential energy. Energy is released when the spring is let go.

Nuclear energy

Nuclear energy is stored in the nucleus (middle) of atoms. Nuclear power stations use this to produce electricity. The light and heat given out by the Sun are produced by nuclear energy.

Electrical energy

Electrical energy travels through electric wires by jumping from atom to atom. It can be turned into many other forms of energy such as sound and light.

1. Which sort of energy does a piece of stretched elastic have?

2. Hot water has more energy than steam. True or false?

Kinetic energy

Kinetic energy is the energy in movement. Everything that moves has kinetic energy. The faster it moves and the heavier it is, the more kinetic energy it has.

3. Can you name two forms of energy that you would find in lightning?

4. The first nuclear power station opened in: a) 1601; b) 1956; c) 1990.

5. Can sound energy travel through walls?

Where does energy come from?

Almost all of the energy on earth comes from the sun. The sun's heat warms the land, sea and air. It also causes the winds, waves and ocean currents, which all have kinetic energy. The energy in food also comes directly from the sun, as shown in the picture.

Plants use sunlight to make their food, which they store as chemical energy in their stems and leaves.

The energy in meat comes from the plants which were eaten by the animal.

Coal, oil and natural gas have formed over millions of years from plant and animal remains. Their energy comes from the chemical energy stored in plants and animals.

6. Manure can be used as a source of energy. True or false?

7. Oil, coal and natural gas are called: a) solid fuels; b) fossil fuels; c) solar fuels.

8. Without the sun, there would be no rain. True or false?

Three main sources of energy do not come directly from the sun's heat and light. These are radioactive materials such as uranium, which are used to make nuclear power; the heat deep within the earth; and tidal energy, which is caused by the pull of the sun and moon on the earth's oceans.

9. Uranium is a type of: a) metal; b) plastic; c) salt.

Where does energy go?

When energy is used, it changes into another form of energy. Energy never goes away and new energy is never made. Even energy that seems to fade to nothing, such as the sound of your voice, is not lost: it just spreads out further and further as tiny vibrations.

Fireworks are stores of chemical energy. When they explode, the chemical energy is suddenly turned into sound, light, heat and kinetic energy.

When a cat pounces, the chemical energy stored within its body is turned into kinetic energy. When animals move, their muscles also produce heat energy.

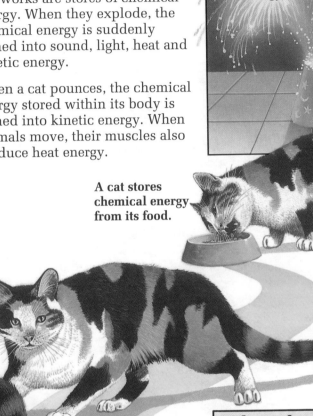

Light energy

Heat energy

Sound energy

Kinetic energy

Chemical energy

A cat stores chemical energy from its food.

Chemical energy is turned into kinetic energy and heat.

How is food turned into energy?

When you eat, food is broken down, or digested, in your stomach and intestines. It is then absorbed into your blood, which is pumped around your body to your muscles.

In your muscles, energy is released from food by a process like very slow burning, called respiration. Respiration, like burning, needs oxygen. This is why you breathe.

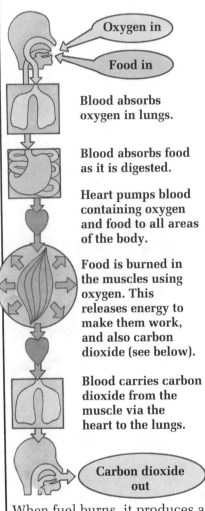

Oxygen in

Food in

Blood absorbs oxygen in lungs.

Blood absorbs food as it is digested.

Heart pumps blood containing oxygen and food to all areas of the body.

Food is burned in the muscles using oxygen. This releases energy to make them work, and also carbon dioxide (see below).

Blood carries carbon dioxide from the muscle via the heart to the lungs.

Carbon dioxide out

When fuel burns, it produces a gas called carbon dioxide. Your blood carries the carbon dioxide produced in your muscles back to your heart, which pumps it to your lungs so you can breathe it out.

Did you know?

Around 70% of the energy in fuels is lost when they are used to produce electricity. This is because some energy escapes as heat each time energy changes form. At a power station, energy has to change three times, from fuel to heat, to movement and then to electricity. Heat escapes at each stage.

10. *What sorts of energy does a burning candle produce?*

11. *Which form of energy cannot travel through space: a) heat; b) light; c) sound?*

12. *Most light bulbs lose 95% of their energy as heat. True or false?*

13. *Energy in food is measured in: a) calories; b) watts; c) grams.*

14. *Who has more stored energy, a fat person or a thin person?*

15. *Do you use energy when you are asleep?*

Electricity and magnetism

Electricity and magnetism are forms of energy, like sound and light. They have an effect on each other that can be put to many uses, from driving an electric motor to powering a computer.

What is electricity?

Electricity is made from electrons: the particles that make up the outside of an atom (see page 69).

In some materials, the electrons can move easily from atom to atom. This flow of electrons is called electricity. It occurs naturally, and it can also be man-made.

Materials that electrons can pass through easily, such as metals, are called conductors. Copper is used in electrical wiring because it is a good conductor. Materials which electrons cannot pass through, such as plastic, are called insulators.

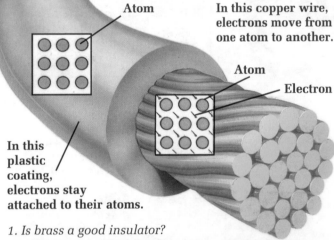

Atom

In this copper wire, electrons move from one atom to another.

Atom

Electron

In this plastic coating, electrons stay attached to their atoms.

1. Is brass a good insulator?

Did you know?

Electricity produces heat and fires can start if electrical wiring overheats. Fire-fighters use foam instead of water to put out electrical fires. This is because water conducts electricity and could give the fire-fighters electric shocks.

How does electricity get to your home?

Electrons do not move along a wire by themselves, they are pushed along by a force. Power stations create this force, which is measured in volts.

Heat from a nuclear reaction, for example, turns water to steam. The steam drives a turbine which spins a magnet in a coil of wire.

2. Are all turbines powered by steam?

This causes an electric current to flow in the coil. This device, called a generator, sends electricity from the power station along a wire cable.

Power station

What causes lightning?

Lightning is caused by static electricity. This is the same kind of electricity as man-made electricity but it is made in a different way. It happens naturally when two materials rub against each other.

3. Thunder is the noise made when lightning hits the ground. True or false?

4. Does lightning hit the highest or lowest point on the ground beneath it?

Lightning occurs when water and air particles in a cloud rub against one another. An electrical force, or charge, builds up and jumps to the earth, or another cloud, in a huge flash.

Cloud

Water rubs against air.

Lightning

5. Which one of the following can be caused by static electricity: a) hair standing up on end; b) fireworks; c) torrential rain?

If you walk on a nylon carpet and drag your feet, electrons jump from the carpet to your feet. This causes an electrical charge to build up on your body. When you touch a metal object, the static electricity jumps over to it, giving you a tiny electric shock.

Nylon carpet

Electrons jump

Electric shock

6. Lightning never strikes in the same place twice. True or false?

7. Tiny electric shocks keep you alive. True or false?

8. Which of these would help prevent electric shocks: a) rubber boots; b) steel helmet; c) cotton socks?

9. Why is it unsafe to use an electrical appliance when your hands are wet?

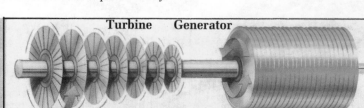

Turbine **Generator**

Flow of electricity

How do magnets work?

In a magnet, there are millions of particles which all have a tiny magnetic force. These particles line up to point the same way, making a force strong enough to pull or push certain metals within the magnet's range, or field.

Only a few metals, such as iron, have magnetic particles. In iron, these particles can be lined up easily to make a magnet. If you hit it with a hammer, the particles no longer line up and the iron loses its magnetic force: it becomes demagnetized.

10. Can magnets pick up wood?

11. Is the Earth magnetic?

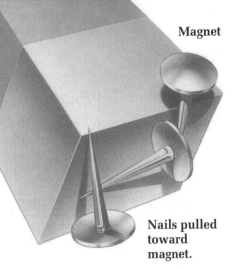

Magnet

Particles in an iron magnet.

Demagnetized particles

Nails pulled toward magnet.

12. Does glue work by magnetism?

How does a junkyard magnet work?

Powerful magnets, which can be switched on and off, are used to move heavy pieces of metal around junkyards. These magnets, called electromagnets, work because an electric current flowing along a wire creates a magnetic field. This effect is called electromagnetism. It is used to work many machines in factories and homes.

An electromagnet is made by coiling electrical wire around a bar of easily magnetized metal, such as iron. When the current is switched on, the magnetism of the metal bar and the wire coil combine.

So, when the operator of a junkyard magnet wants to pick up metal, the magnet is switched on. The operator can then move the metal by swinging the giant magnet. When the operator wants to drop the metal, the current is switched off.

Electrical wire coiled around magnet.

13. Electrical power is measured in: a) Whys; b) Sparks; c) Watts.

How does an electric motor work?

If a coil of wire is put inside a magnetic field and the current switched on, the coil is attracted by the magnetic field around it, which makes it spin. The spin of the wire coil can drive a machine. This device is called an electric motor. Electric motors are used in many machines such as an electric fan, or a food blender.

Magnet

Spindle turns blades.

Wire coil

Blades turn, circulating air in the room.

14. Which one of these electric devices uses an electric motor: a) kettle; b) light bulb; c) doorbell; d) washing machine?

15. Electric motors were invented in: a) 1421; b) 1621; c) 1821.

At home, electricity is fed into a meter which records how much is used. It also flows through a fuse, a narrow wire which melts if the current is too strong.

The wires and machines that electricity flows through are called a circuit. All parts of a circuit must connect for electricity to flow.

Switches control electricity in the circuit. Switching on or off completes or breaks the circuit, working a radio, for example.

Meter

Fuse

Switch

On

Off

Sound and music

Sound is a kind of energy which travels through air, water and solid objects such as walls and the ground. Most types of sound contain only a small amount of energy.

How are sounds made?

Sounds happen when the tiny particles that make up the air are made to move back and forth very quickly. This movement is called vibration.

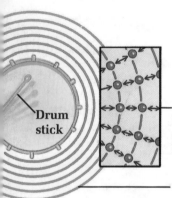

When a drum is hit, the skin vibrates and bumps into air particles.

Drum stick

Air particles bump into the ones next to them.

Sound travels as waves of vibrating air.

The waves travel in an expanding circle. Strong vibrations make loud noises and gentle ones make quiet noises.

1. Which has more energy, the sound of a handclap or a clap of thunder?

2. The loudness of a sound is measured in: a) handbels; b) loudbels; c) decibels.

3. Can sound travel around corners?

What makes sounds different?

When air particles vibrate quickly, the sound waves travel close together. You hear them as a high-pitched sound, such as a bird's chirrup.

If air particles vibrate slowly, the sound waves are further apart. You hear them as a low-pitched sound, such as the chugging of a truck. The speed of vibration is called frequency.

What is an echo?

When sound waves hit a solid surface, such as a cliff, some travel through it. Others bounce back, like waves in the sea bouncing back off the cliff.

Sound waves travel back through the air towards the source of the original sound. You then hear the sound again, as an echo. Short, loud noises make the best echoes.

Fishing boats find schools of fish by sending high-pitched sounds down into the sea. The sounds echo back off the fish, and a computer onboard interprets the echoes, locating the fish.

7. Can children hear higher frequencies than adults?

8. Would you hear an echo better on a windy day or a calm day?

High-frequency sound

Low-frequency sound

Sound   Echo

9. Some sounds are so loud they are able to travel around the world. True or false?

10. Locating objects by listening to echoes of high-frequency sound is called: a) radar; b) sonar; c) laser.

How do you hear?

Your ears pick up vibrations in the air, and turn them into electrical signals that your brain can understand.

The outside flap is called the pinna. It helps to funnel the vibrations toward the eardrum.

The eardrum vibrates when sounds hit it.

4. The bones in the middle ear are called the nut, bolt and screw. True or false?

Three tiny bones pick up the vibrations. These bones carry the vibrations to the inner ear.

The vibrations go into a spiral tube full of liquid, called the cochlea. Nerves change vibrations into electrical signals and carry them to your brain.

Nerves

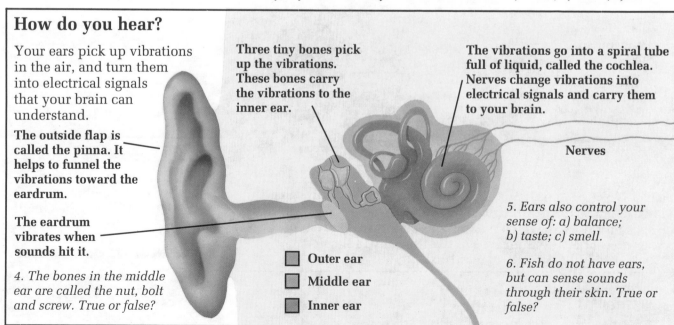

☐ Outer ear
☐ Middle ear
☐ Inner ear

5. Ears also control your sense of: a) balance; b) taste; c) smell.

6. Fish do not have ears, but can sense sounds through their skin. True or false?

What sounds do animals hear?

Many large animals, such as elephants, can hear lower sounds than people, but not the high sounds that we do. Many small animals, such as shrews and bats, can hear and make higher sounds than people. Bats listen to the echoes of the sounds they make, to find insects to eat.

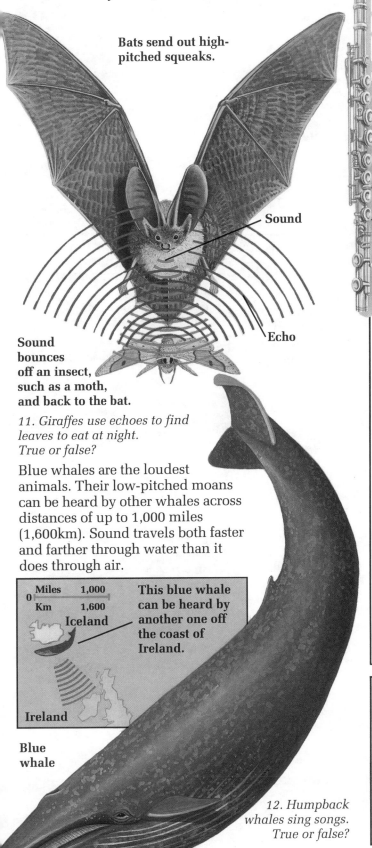

Bats send out high-pitched squeaks.

Sound

Echo

Sound bounces off an insect, such as a moth, and back to the bat.

11. Giraffes use echoes to find leaves to eat at night. True or false?

Blue whales are the loudest animals. Their low-pitched moans can be heard by other whales across distances of up to 1,000 miles (1,600km). Sound travels both faster and farther through water than it does through air.

Miles	1,000
0	
Km	1,600

Iceland

This blue whale can be heard by another one off the coast of Ireland.

Ireland

Blue whale

12. Humpback whales sing songs. True or false?

What makes instruments sound different?

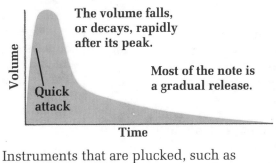

Musical instruments sound different because they make vibrations in different ways. Their shape, the materials they are made of, and how they are played, affect the way that they vibrate. This gives each instrument its own range of notes and its own distinctive tone.

Musical notes all have a similar pattern. They begin, build up to full volume and then fade away. The time that each stage takes depends on the instrument and the way the player controls the note. The graph below shows an example of the shape of a flute note.

The length of time the note stays at its loudest is called the sustain.

Volume

The start of the note is called the attack.

The fade of the note is called the release.

Time

Flute

Wind instruments, such as the flute, have a fairly quick attack and release. The note sustains for as long as the player blows. The graph below shows the shape of another note, played on a guitar.

The volume falls, or decays, rapidly after its peak.

Volume

Most of the note is a gradual release.

Quick attack

Time

Instruments that are plucked, such as the guitar, have a quick attack and no sustain. There is a long release as the string gradually stops vibrating.

13. Drums, cymbals and xylophones are all: a) percussion instruments; b) percolated instruments; c) polystyrene instruments.

14. Unravel each of these words to make the names of four instruments: angor, batu, napio, tirgua.

Guitar

Did you know?

There are no sounds in space. This is because there is no air for sound waves to travel through. Without air, water or solid particles to vibrate, there is no noise. In space, astronauts talk to each other by radio.

15. Any place, such as outer space, where there is no air is called: a) air-tight; b) arid; c) a vacuum.

Light and color

Light is a form of energy that enables us to see the things around us. It is released by sources of heat, such as the sun, a light bulb or a candle.

Light is made up of seven different colors — red, orange, yellow, green, blue, indigo and violet. These colors normally merge together, so that you cannot see them separately.

What is a rainbow?

Light travels in waves and the wavelengths of the seven colors are all slightly different. A rainbow appears when the colors are split apart.

Light waves are so small that around 40 thousand of them would fit in this wavelength here.

Wavelength

If light enters a transparent substance (such as glass or water) directly, it travels straight through. However, if it enters at an angle, it bends. This is called refraction. At some angles, the seven colors all bend in a slightly different direction, so you can see them all. This is called dispersion.

You can see this effect if you shine light through a triangular glass block, called a prism. The prism is shaped to refract and disperse light.

Rainbows happen when the sun shines while it is raining, or just after a shower. Sunlight travels through the raindrops and is refracted and dispersed.

Each color travels in a slightly different direction.

Prism

Light

48

Red
Orange
Yellow
Green
Blue
Indigo
Violet

How do you see color?

When light waves hit objects, they bounce back. This is called reflection. Objects appear to be different colors because they reflect some of the colors in light and absorb others. When light shines on an object, the reflected colors bounce back into your eyes.

This T-shirt is black because it absorbs all the colors in light. It reflects hardly any light.

This plant appears green because it only reflects green light and no other colors.

This rabbit appears white because it reflects all the colors in white light equally well.

4. All animals see in black-and-white. True or false?
5. Some animals make light. True or false?
6. What colors does snow reflect?

What makes the sky blue?

When sunlight hits the Earth's atmosphere, it begins to break up and blue light is scattered all over the sky. This happens because the upper atmosphere contains gas and dust particles which are about the same size as the wavelength of blue light. This causes blue light to bounce off them.

The atmosphere gets thicker the nearer it is to the Earth's surface, and as light travels through it, more light is scattered. Light with shorter wavelengths, like blue and violet are scattered most.

At sunset or sunrise, sunlight travels through much more of the atmosphere before it reaches you. Most of its colors are scattered by the time it reaches the lower atmosphere. Only reds and oranges are left.

At midday, blue light is scattered over the sky.

7. The sea is blue because: a) it contains blue seaweed; b) squid squirt blue dye; c) it reflects the sky.

8. Can light travel through space?

At sunset, only red and orange light can be seen.

1. If red and yellow are mixed together, do they make: a) blue; b) green; c) orange?

2. Another name for the colors of the rainbow is: a) a spatula; b) a spectrum; c) a sporran.

How does a mirror work?

Light waves reflect in a similar way to a ball bouncing. For example, when a tennis ball hits a smooth clay court, it bounces evenly, leaving the surface of the court at the same angle at which it arrived. Light behaves like this when it hits a mirror. It travels through a smooth, glass layer and then bounces off a shiny, metal coating. Light waves all bounce back evenly, staying in the same order, which enables you to see a reflection.

If you play tennis on an uneven surface such as grass, balls hitting different bumps will bounce at different angles. Light behaves like this when it hits a dull, rough surface, such as wood. Light rays scatter in all directions.

9. Ancient Egyptians used mirrors. True or false?

10. Can you see a reflection in polished wood?

The ball bounces back at the same angle that it hits the clay.

Light remains in same order.

The ball bounces back at a different angle than at which it hits the grass.

Light is scattered.

How do you see?

You see objects because light bounces off them and reflects into your eyes. This picture shows how what you see is turned into an image that your brain can recognize. Light enters through the pupil, a black hole at the front of the eye. The colored area around the pupil, the iris, prevents harmful light rays from entering the eye. Light then passes through a transparent, rubbery disc, called a lens.

The lens helps you see more clearly, or focus, by bending light, so that it hits the back of the eye, which is called the retina. The lens turns what you see upside down. The retina is made up of millions of tiny cells that are called rods and cones. Rods are sensitive to dim light. Cones are sensitive to bright light and color. There are over 130 million rods and cones in an eye. When light falls on them, electrical messages are passed to the optic nerve.

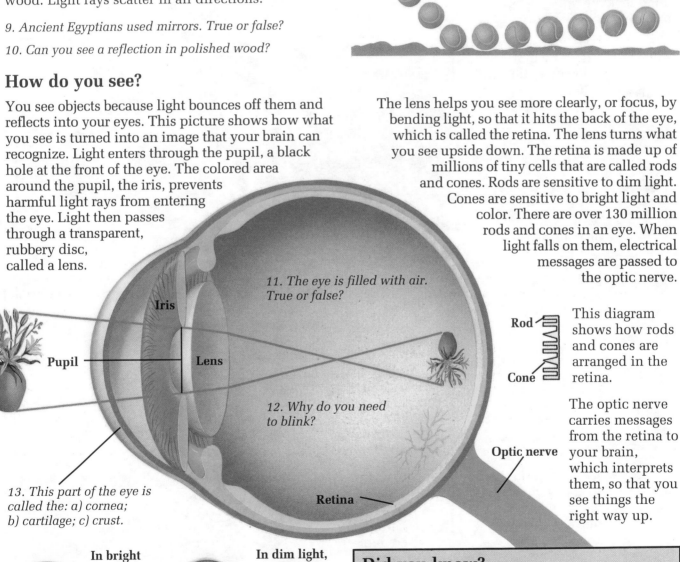

Iris

11. The eye is filled with air. True or false?

Pupil

Lens

12. Why do you need to blink?

Rod

Cone

This diagram shows how rods and cones are arranged in the retina.

The optic nerve carries messages from the retina to your brain, which interprets them, so that you see things the right way up.

Optic nerve

Retina

13. This part of the eye is called the: a) cornea; b) cartilage; c) crust.

In bright light, the iris closes up to protect your eyes.

In dim light, the iris opens up to let more light in, so you can see better.

Did you know?

Light travels quicker than anything in the universe. Its speed is around 186,000 miles (300,000km) per second. This means that it takes eight minutes to travel the 93 million miles(150 million km) from the sun to earth.

15. Which travels faster, thunder or lightning?

14. Which two of these animals can see well in the dark: a) dogs; b) cats; c) owls; d) sheep; e) ducks?

Living things

There is life in almost every part of the world. The sky, sea, soil and surface of the earth are full of plants and animals.

What makes something a living thing?

Living things have particular features which non-living things lack. For instance, they can react to their surroundings, they need energy to live and can reproduce. Below you can see the qualities which separate living things from non-living things.

Leaf cells

All living things are made up of tiny units, called cells.

All living things need oxygen, which they get from air or water.

The bodies of living things produce waste, which they need to get rid of.

All animals can move part of their bodies. Flowers can open and close petals.

Almost all living things grow. Growth occurs when cells divide.

All living things reproduce so that new ones live on when they die.

All living things need food to give them energy to breed, move or grow.

All living things are aware of their surroundings and react to them.

1. Which one of the following do plants not do: a) reproduce; b) make food; c) think; d) move?

2. An erupting volcano is a living thing. True or false?

What is the difference between an animal and a plant?

Here is how plants and animals differ.

Food

The main difference between plants and animals is the way in which they get their food.

Animals eat plants or other animals, or both. The food is broken down in their bodies and gives them energy. This breakdown of food is called digestion.

3. This animal is a: a) sloth; b) orang-utan; c) lemur.

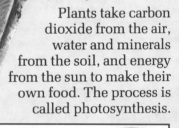

Plants take carbon dioxide from the air, water and minerals from the soil, and energy from the sun to make their own food. The process is called photosynthesis.

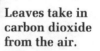

Leaves take in carbon dioxide from the air.

The sun's energy turns carbon dioxide and water into simple sugars.

Cells

The cells in animals' bodies have soft walls.

Animal cell

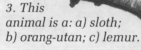

Plant cells have thick, tough walls.

Plant cell

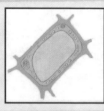

Movement

Most animals can move their bodies around. They are more sensitive than plants and can react quickly to change.

Most plants can only respond slowly to changes. Some turn to follow the sun around the sky, for example.

4. Is a stick insect a plant or an animal?

5. Some plants can eat animals. True or false?

6. Do you know what the yellow flowered plants above are called?

7. Plants always grow away from the sun. True or false?

What are you made of ?

Your body is made of millions of cells, which can reproduce, grow and feed. Cells contain a lot of water; in fact, two-thirds of your body is made of water. The body organs are all made of different kinds of cells. Each has a particular job to do.

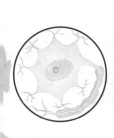

The brain is made of nerve cells. Nerve cells elsewhere in your body send messages to your brain, which tells your body how to react.

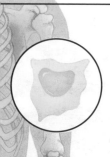

Bone cells make a hard skeleton, which gives your body shape.

8. Which of these is not a bone: a) femur; b) pelvis; c) pancreas?

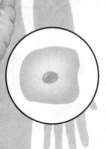

Some cells are only found in one part of the body. The stomach and intestines have digestive cells which produce juices to break down, or digest, food.

Muscle cells squeeze tight and then relax so you can move different parts of your body.

9. Is your brain a muscle?

Did you know?

The stomach produces strong digestive juices. It is lined with mucus, a sticky substance, which protects it from being eaten away by its own juices.

Where do you come from?

All human beings, and most other animals, begin as just two cells, one from the mother (the egg cell), and one from the father (the sperm cell). These two cells join together to make one cell. This cell then divides into two and each of those cells divides again. This process continues and the number of cells increases. As the baby grows within the mother's womb, specialized cells begin to form the baby's body organs.

After a baby has been born, it continues to grow. Growing bodies need a lot of a certain substance made by the cells, called protein. When you eat food rich in protein, such as cheese, the body absorbs it and the cells use it to make their own protein.

10. In the womb, a baby is attached to its mother by the: a) umbilical cord; b) major chord; c) spinal cord.

11. Which is bigger, an egg cell or a sperm cell?

Why do you stop growing?

Your body grows longer and larger as the bones of your skeleton grow. A group of cells near the brain, called the pituitary gland, produce chemicals which control how much you grow. When the pituitary gland stops making these chemicals, you stop growing.

Growth occurs in three main spurts: in the first two years, between five and seven, and between twelve and eighteen.

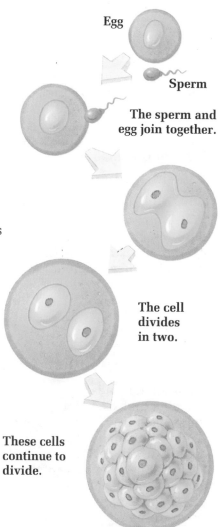

Egg

Sperm

The sperm and egg join together.

The cell divides in two.

These cells continue to divide.

12. Which one of these types of food is essential for growth: a) fat; b) sugar; c) protein?

13. You are taller first thing in the morning than last thing at night. True or false?

14. Human skeletons have over 200 bones. True or false?

15. Which one of the following never stops growing while you are alive: a) nails; b) teeth; c) feet?

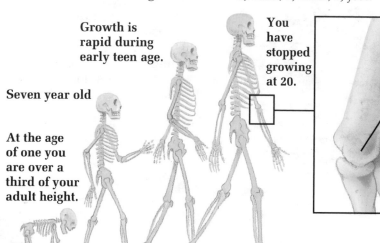

Growth is rapid during early teen age.

You have stopped growing at 20.

Bones grow here, just behind the ends.

Seven year old

At the age of one you are over a third of your adult height.

Evolution

When living things reproduce, their offspring look similar to them. However, living things can change their appearance if their environment changes. For example, if it gradually gets colder, over many generations, a species of animal may grow a thicker and thicker coat. This change is called evolution. Over millions of years, these changes can make a new plant or animal which may be quite different from its ancestor.

1. Cats have evolved from dogs. True or false?

How does evolution work?

Evolution depends on a process called natural selection, which works like this. All animals and plants within one species are slightly different. Some of these differences enable some of the species to survive better than others. For example, a deer that can outrun predators successfully will be more likely to survive to reproduce. Its running abilities may be passed on to, or inherited by, its offspring.

Evolution has produced countless ways of coping with the hazards of life on Earth. For example, the horse chestnut has evolved a spiky covering for its seeds.

The spikes protect the seed when it falls from the tree.

2. Are horse chestnut seeds edible?

3. Would animals with short lifespans and many offspring evolve quicker than those with long lifespans and one or two offspring?

How quick is evolution?

Evolution is usually very slow, but in some cases one type of animal can change very quickly rather than over thousands or millions of years. For example, over the last two hundred years, peppered moths have evolved by changing color, to fit into areas of Europe that have a lot of heavy industry.

Most peppered moths used to have pale wings. They rested on pale tree trunks where they were well hidden. About 1% of them had dark wings. These were easily spotted by birds, and were usually eaten.

About 200 years ago, coal-powered factories were built in western Europe. Smoke from factory steam engines began to blacken tree trunks with soot. The pale moths then became easier to spot.

The few dark moths survived as they were not seen by the birds. They then produced more dark-winged offspring. Now most peppered moths in industrial areas have dark wings.

4. Do moths usually come out during the day or the night?

Why do some animals become extinct?

Some living things are not able to evolve when their environment changes, so they die out. Large, hairy, elephant-like animals called mammoths probably became extinct because the earth's climate became more extreme. It became too hot in summer and too cold in winter. Also, human hunters had reduced their numbers. Saber-toothed tigers became extinct because their huge fangs were only suitable for hunting large animals, such as mammoths. They were not able to hunt the smaller animals that remained, so they died out.

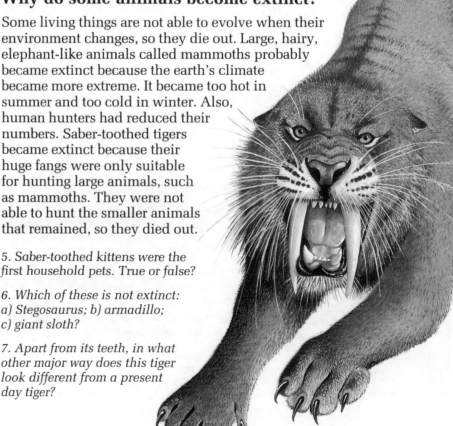

5. Saber-toothed kittens were the first household pets. True or false?

6. Which of these is not extinct: a) Stegosaurus; b) armadillo; c) giant sloth?

7. Apart from its teeth, in what other major way does this tiger look different from a present day tiger?

How do we know humans have evolved?

Most scientists think that humans have evolved from tree-living animals similar to apes and monkeys. There is evidence in our bodies that supports this view, and suggests that we used to live on a vegetarian diet of fruit, roots and stems.

At the base of the spine there is a set of bones called the coccyx. This is all that remains of what used to be a tail.

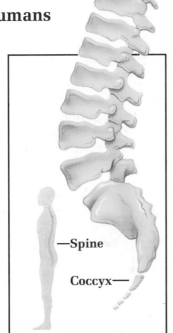

—Spine

Coccyx—

Most of your body hair is downy, but it used to be much thicker. Each hair has a muscle to make it stand up if you are cold. On hairy mammals this traps air which keeps them warm.

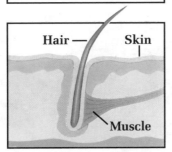

Hair — Skin

—Muscle

Many adults still have large back teeth called wisdom teeth. These are no longer necessary, but were originally needed to chew the tough vegetables our ancestors used to eat.

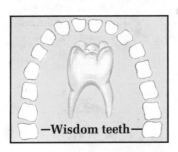

—Wisdom teeth—

The appendix is a small tube attached to the intestine. Your distant ancestors needed it to help digest their vegetable diet. It is no longer needed and is slowly getting smaller.

Plant-eating animals, such as rabbits, have a particularly well-developed appendix.

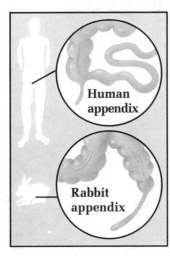

Human appendix

Rabbit appendix

8. Are wisdom teeth only found in intelligent people?

9. People have eyebrows to: a) keep sweat out of their eyes; b) trap insects; c) keep their eyes warm.

10. Most scientists think that the first humans lived in: a) Antarctica; b) Africa; c) Argentina.

Can people control evolution?

People have been controlling animal evolution for over 10,000 years. For example, most breeds of dog today probably evolved from the wolves which used to gather around early human settlements. Gradually, the wolves that came to live with humans evolved into a separate species, dogs. Humans began to breed them for particular tasks. This is called selective breeding. There are now over 150 breeds of dog.

Dogs that could learn to obey human calls, such as this Old English sheepdog, were bred to herd animals.

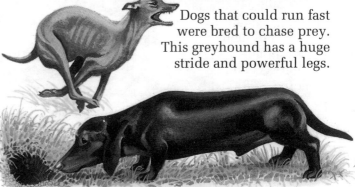

Dogs that could run fast were bred to chase prey. This greyhound has a huge stride and powerful legs.

Dogs with a good sense of smell were bred to track down prey. This smooth-haired dachshund can burrow into rabbit warrens.

Natural selection and evolution are usually very slow. Selective breeding is much faster.

11. Dogs that are from one particular breed are called: a) pedigree dogs; b) pedestal dogs; c) perennial dogs.

12. Which of these dogs looks most like a wolf: a) boxer; b) terrier; c) husky?

13. Are lions the product of selective breeding?

14. Which animal is a cross between a donkey and a horse?

What is genetic engineering?

In the 1970s, scientists discovered how to change the character of a living thing by altering its genes. This is called genetic engineering. Genes, a biological recipe contained in every cell, also determine the size and appearance of a living thing. Genetic engineering can be used to breed plants and animals that grow bigger, or are more resistant to disease.

15. Genetic engineering is a branch of which science: a) botany; b) bionics; c) biotechnology?

The balance of nature

Everything in nature is linked together in a delicate balance. When a plant or animal dies, it becomes food for other living things, so nothing is wasted. People can disturb this balance by taking too much from nature for food and industry, and by polluting their environment.

1. The study of living things in their environment is called economics. True or false?

2. Protecting the environment is called: a) conurbation; b) conservation; c) contamination.

How does the sun provide energy?

Plants need energy from the sun in order to make their food, in a process called photosynthesis.* Plants provide energy for the animals that eat them. These animals are then eaten by other animals. This transfer of energy from the sun through plants to animals is called a food chain. A typical food chain is shown here.

3. Do hawks hunt by day or by night?

Beetle eats plant.   **Thrush eats beetle.**   **Hawk eats thrush.**

What is a food web?

Most animals eat a variety of food, and what they eat affects the other plants and animals in their environment. Scientists call this feeding relationship a food web. Here is the kind of food web you would find in a forest environment. In any food web there are millions of plant-eating animals at the bottom of the web, but only a few animals at the top.

4. Which has more choice of food, the owl or the thrush?

5. Which animal does the rabbit need to watch out for?

6. All large animals are carnivores. True or false?

7. Are humans carnivores, herbivores or omnivores?

8. Would there be more hawks or more caterpillars in a forest food web?

*9. Which of these is a real beetle:
a) Boiling beetle;
b) Boring beetle;
c) Bouzouki beetle?*

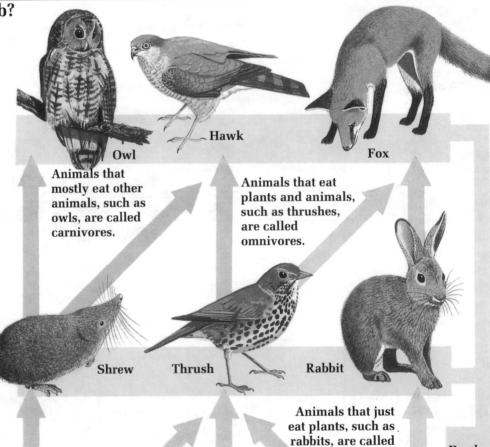

Owl **Hawk** **Fox**

Animals that mostly eat other animals, such as owls, are called carnivores.

Animals that eat plants and animals, such as thrushes, are called omnivores.

Shrew **Thrush** **Rabbit**

Animals that just eat plants, such as rabbits, are called herbivores.

Dead plants and animals add goodness to the soil.

Beetle **Caterpillar** **Berry**

Can food webs be damaged?

Because living things in a food web feed on each other, poisoning or removing one plant or animal will affect many others. Here are three ways in which food webs can be damaged.

Large areas of tropical rainforest are cleared every day to make land for farming. Without dead plants and animals to enrich the forest soil it becomes too poor to produce food.

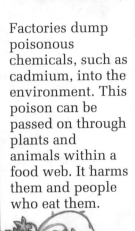

Factories dump poisonous chemicals, such as cadmium, into the environment. This poison can be passed on through plants and animals within a food web. It harms them and people who eat them.

If a type of animal disappears from an area, the animals that eat it are affected. For example, many sea birds have far less food because the sand eels they eat have been caught and turned into farm animal food.

How can you protect your environment?

See if you can reuse items you might usually throw away. Much household waste can also be taken to recycling points if you collect it separately.

Paper can be used to make new paper, cardboard and tissue. It can also be used for insulation.

Bottles can be cleaned and used again. Glass can be melted down and made into new bottles.

Many metal goods, such as drink cans, can be recycled.

Plastic bags can be reused several times. However, most plastics cannot be recycled.

What happens to the waste that people produce?

The recycling that occurs in nature does not exist in most human societies. Waste from homes and factories cannot be absorbed back into the environment.

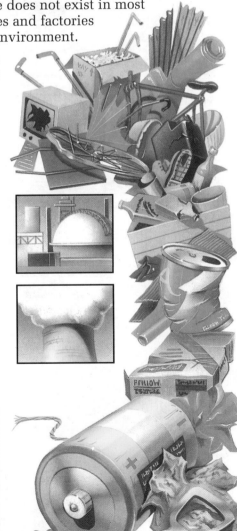

Most waste from homes and shops is buried in the ground. Soil keeps it in place, keeps out scavengers, and stops the smell.

10. Sites where waste is buried are called: a) landfills; b) subways; c) grottoes.

Nuclear power stations make waste which remains dangerous for centuries. The waste is set in concrete and stored underground or dumped in the sea.

11. Which Ukrainian nuclear power station caused widespread pollution when it exploded in 1986?

Waste from factories is often poisonous. Some factories dispose of their waste carefully, but many others pollute the air, land and water in their environment.

Rotting vegetables and fruit make a substance called compost, which contains a lot of goodness. It can be dug into your garden.

Rags can be used by industry to make items such as roof felt or furniture stuffing.

12. Can iron be recycled?

13. Compost heaps take about: a) a week; b) a month; c) six months to rot.

14. Materials that rot are called: a) biographical; b) biodegradable; c) diabolical.

15. The average North American home throws away over a ton (tonne) of waste every year. True or false?

Did you know?

Pollution is not a new problem. In 1306 King Edward I of England complained of the "unbearable stench" caused by burning coal in London, and prohibited its use.

Science and technology

Using scientific ideas in a practical way is called technology. Scientists develop new technology to sell products and to improve your lifestyle. Here are some examples of where technology has been used to create new electrical equipment and new products to help protect the environment.

How do compact discs store music?

When music is recorded for a compact disc (CD), a computer measures the sound wave 40,000 times per second. These measurements are converted into a number system called binary code. In this system, all numbers are represented by a combination of the digits zero and one.

A computer measures the height and shape of the wave, as shown by the red arrows. These measurements describe the wave's shape.

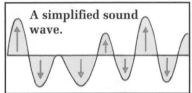
A simplified sound wave.

The CD surface has a sequence of millions of pits and flat areas, representing a digital code. Pits are read as zero. Flat areas are read as one.

Inside the computer, binary numbers are represented by patterns of electrical pulses: a pulse stands for the digit one, and no pulse stands for the digit zero. This way of coding information as a pattern of pulses is called digital coding. Recording music in this way is very accurate, giving excellent sound quality on the CD.

The digital code is cut into the shiny surface of the CD in a sequence of pits and flat areas, representing zeros and ones. In the CD player, an extremely strong beam of light, called a laser, is shone on the disc as it spins. When light hits a flat area, it is reflected. When it hits a pit, it is not reflected.

The CD player interprets these reflections as a series of on and off signals, which make up the digital code of the recorded sound. The code is then converted back by a reverse process into the sound waves of the original piece of music.

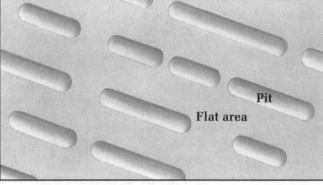

Pit

Flat area

1. CDs are coated with a protective layer of: a) paper; b) plastic; c) marble.

2. Is music the only kind of information that can be stored on CD?

3. The picture above has been magnified around: a) 8 times; b) 80 times; c) 8,000 times.

4. CDs wear out if they are played several times a day. True or false?

Did you know?

Unlike daylight, laser light is made up of only one wavelength. Its waves do not scatter, but travel together in one direction. This makes it so strong that some lasers can cut through metal. Lasers were invented in 1960, but for years no one knew what to do with them. They now have many uses, such as in eye surgery, where they are used to make fine, precise cuts.

Laser beam

5. Lasers are used in supermarkets. True or false?

6. Can lasers measure distances?

7. Laser light can be brighter than the sun. True or false?

Can car pollution be reduced?

Car exhaust fumes contain poisonous chemicals which cause air pollution. To reduce this, all new cars that use unleaded fuel can be fitted with a machine called a catalytic converter, which cleans exhaust gases. As exhaust gases flow through the converter, they pass over a surface covered with metal atoms. These make the chemicals in the gas react to make less harmful gases.

EXHAUST FUMES IN	EXHAUST FUMES OUT
Carbon monoxide	Carbon dioxide
Nitrogen oxides	Nitrogen
Hydrocarbons	Water

Catalytic converter: palladium, platinum and rhodium atoms.

8. How many new cars in the USA are fitted with catalytic converters: a) none; b) half; c) all of them?

9. Can exhaust fumes cause acid rain?

10. Breathing carbon monoxide makes your hair turn white. True or false?

How can light bulbs save energy?

When the metal wire in a light bulb glows, it produces heat as well as light. Producing this heat wastes electrical energy.

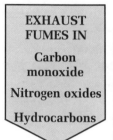

Energy efficient light bulbs

An energy efficient bulb makes light with chemicals instead of heat. Inside the bulb is a folded fluorescent tube. When electricity passes through it, chemicals glow, giving off light.

11. Energy efficient light bulbs last: a) 8; b) 30; c) 150 times as long as ordinary bulbs.

12. Energy efficient bulbs can only light up in the dark. True or false?

How does a camcorder work?

A camcorder is a mini combination of two machines – a TV camera and a video recorder. It works by using lenses to create an image on a tiny light-sensitive electronic component called a charge-coupled device (CCD).

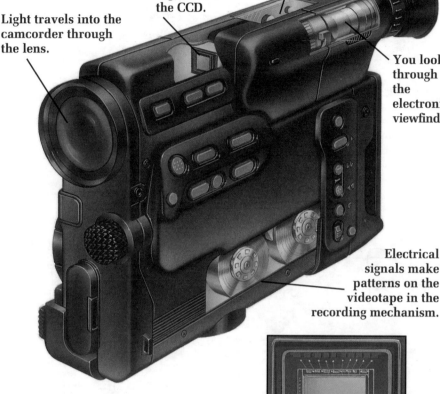

Light travels into the camcorder through the lens.

Light hits the CCD.

Electronic circuits send electrical signals to the recording mechanism.

You look through the electronic viewfinder.

Electrical signals make patterns on the videotape in the recording mechanism.

Charge-coupled device (CCD) magnified 1.85 times.

13. What does camcorder stand for?

The CCD is divided into a grid of tiny squares, called pixels, which are coated with a light-sensitive chemical. When light hits the CCD, it generates an electrical signal, which corresponds to the amount of light hitting it. Bright light produces a strong signal and dim light produces a weak signal.

These electrical signals travel to the recording mechanism. Here, the electrical signals create a magnetic field* which makes a pattern on magnetic particles on the surface of a plastic videotape.

The patterns on the tape store the picture information represented by the electrical signals. The sound is recorded on a separate area of the videotape. The tape can then be played back through the camcorder itself or through a video recorder.

Cutaway of video cassette, to show tape inside.

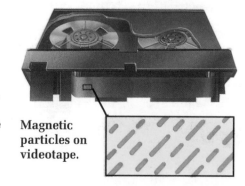

Magnetic particles on videotape.

14. There are about 400,000 pixels on the CCD. True or false?

15. What is a palmcorder?

*See pages 44-45 for more about electricity and magnetism. **57**

Science Megaquiz

These ten quizzes test you on what you have read in Part Two of this book, and also on your general knowledge of science.

You can write your answers on a piece of paper and then check on page 64 to see how many you got right.

Misfits

In each set of three below, there is one misfit. Can you spot which it is?

1.	2.	3.	4.	5.	6.	7.	8.	9.	10.
pupil	kinetic	gravity	violet	light bulb	growth	cat	proton	egg	flute
iris	original	friction	brown	turbine	feeding	greyhound	electron	baby	xylophone
pinna	chemical	density	indigo	generator	magnetism	mammoth	siphon	sperm	drum

Inventions and discoveries

Can you match these inventions and discoveries to their dates?

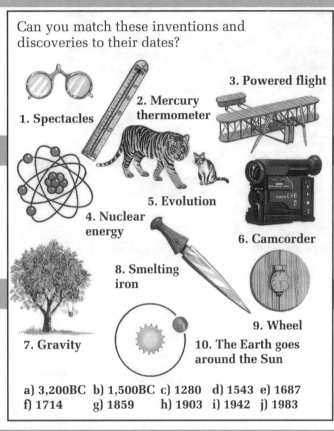

1. Spectacles
2. Mercury thermometer
3. Powered flight
4. Nuclear energy
5. Evolution
6. Camcorder
7. Gravity
8. Smelting iron
9. Wheel
10. The Earth goes around the Sun

a) 3,200BC b) 1,500BC c) 1280 d) 1543 e) 1687
f) 1714   g) 1859   h) 1903 i) 1942 j) 1983

Talking science

Each of these sentences is missing a word. The missing words are highlighted in the box below. Can you match the words and sentences?

1. At ....., the sky may appear orange and red.
2. Rotting fruit and vegetables can be used to make.....
3. Gold, silicon and oxygen are all ......
4. The earth is surrounded by its own magnetic ....., with a north and a south pole.
5. A ..... splits light into the different colours of the rainbow.
6. All animals and plants in an environment are linked to each other by a ..... web.
7. ..... is the force which pulls you to the ground.
8. Our solar system is part of a ..... called the Milky Way.
9. Acid rain causes ..... in many places, including lakes, forests and cities.
10. Plastic is a good ..... of electricity.

food	prism	compost

sunset	field	galaxy	insulator

gravity	elements	pollution

Materials

1. Which material is the best conductor of electricity: a) air; b) wood; c) metal?
2. Name one harmful substance that may be found in car exhaust fumes.
3. Which raw material is different from the others: a) ore; b) coal; c) trees; d) clay?
4. Is water a compound or an element?
5. Where does suede come from?
6. In the past, what precious metal did alchemists try to make?
7. Which gas is the sun made out of?
8. The cells of living things contain which material: a) oil; b) water; c) blood?
9. Which metal is used in electrical wiring?
10. Which of these raw materials is not used to make energy: a) cocoa; b) coal; c) clay; d) oil?

Close-ups

These are all close-ups of pictures in Part Two. Can you recognize what they are?

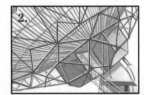

Animals and plants

Which of these living things...

1. ...do thrushes eat?
2. ...is the loudest animal in the world?
3. ...reflects all the colors in sunlight?
4. ...comes from a horse chestnut tree?
5. ...uses echoes to find insects to eat?
6. ...is extinct?
7. ...was bred to herd animals?
8. ...is the nearest animal relative to a chimpanzee and a gorilla?
9. ...eats sand eels?
10. ...lives in a warren?

True or false?

1. When you look at the stars you are looking back in time.
2. Green plants scare caterpillars away.
3. All metals are magnetic.
4. Daylight is a mixture of colors.
5. Two-thirds of your body is water.
6. Stomach cells have teeth.
7. Tiny particles exist which are smaller than an atom.
8. Telephones are connected by cables containing bundles of string.
9. Foxes are herbivores.
10. Sound travels in waves.

Silhouettes

All these silhouettes are things that appear in Part Two. How many can you recognize?

Body bits

Which part or parts of your body...

1. ...carries oxygen around your body?
2. ...do you no longer need to digest food?
3. ...produces chemicals which control how much you grow?
4. ...carries signals from your eye to your brain?
5. ...covers your whole body?
6. ...enables you to move by squeezing tight and relaxing?
7. ...gives your body its shape?
8. ...opens or closes, to let more or less light into your eye when it is bright or dark?
9. ...is all that is left of a tail?
10. ...directs sounds into your eardrum?

What do you know?

1. By what process do plants make food?
2. What kind of electricity is lightning?
3. What does CD stand for?
4. Is it possible to see atoms?
5. How many millions of years ago did the Big Bang happen: a) 15 thousand; b) fifty; c) five?
6. What are rocks which contain metals called?
7. What force, apart from electricity, makes an electric motor work?
8. Which material is not made from oil: a) polythene; b) silk; c) acrylic; d) nylon?
9. What sort of light could cut through metal?
10. Are animals or plants at the bottom of a food web?

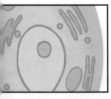    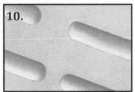

Quiz answers

The answers to the 12 quizzes from *Exploring space* to *Science and technology* are on the next four pages. Give yourself one point for every right answer. The chart below helps you to find out how well you have done.

0-5	Read through the answers, then try the quiz again. See how many answers you can remember this time.
6-10	Quite good. Think more carefully about the questions and you might get more right.

11-14	Good score. If you get this score on most of the quizzes, you have done very well.
15	Excellent. If you do this well in more than half of the quizzes, you are a science genius!

Your score overall

You can find out your average score over all 12 quizzes like this:

1. Add up your scores on all 12 quizzes.
2. Divide this total by 12. This is your average score. How well did you do?

General knowledge

All the answers to general knowledge questions are marked ★. These questions are probably the hardest in the quizzes. Add up how many of them you got right across all 12 quizzes. There are 50 of them in total. If you got over 30 right, your science general knowledge is good.

Exploring space

1. a) Venus, Neptune and Mars are named after Roman gods.
★ 2. Sirius, Betelgeuse and Alpha Centauri are stars.
3. a) Radio waves from stars contain blips, bleeps and hisses.
4. False. Telescopes were first used around 1600, by scientists such as Galileo.

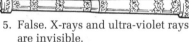

Galileo used a telescope to help him draw pictures of the moon.

5. False. X-rays and ultra-violet rays are invisible.
6. c) A group of stars is called a constellation.
7. True. Scientists believe that in 5,000 million years time, the sun will use up all its fuel and stop shining.
★ 8. No. It is not safe because the sun is too bright and may hurt your eyes.
9. b) You would find a white dwarf in space. When the fuel in a star is used up, it shrinks and becomes a very dense, planet-like mass, called a white dwarf.
10. b) Apollo 11 landed the first men on the Moon in 1969.
11. True. Dogs were sent up into space on experimental space flights.
12. True. Many ships carry equipment that uses information from satellites to tell them exactly where they are.
13. a) The word "satellite" comes from the Latin word for attendant.
★ 14. The former Soviet Union launched the first satellite in 1957.

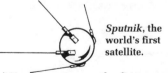

***Sputnik*, the world's first satellite.**

15. b) Yuri Gagarin was the first man to go into space, in April 1961.

What are things made of?

★ 1. Mercury used to be called quicksilver. It is a silvery metal, but it is a liquid at room temperature.
2. True. Diamonds and coal are both made from carbon atoms. The carbon atoms fit together in different ways.

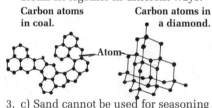

Carbon atoms in coal. **Carbon atoms in a diamond.** Atom

3. c) Sand cannot be used for seasoning food.
★ 4. Water is always ice at the North and South Poles, where the temperature never rises above freezing point.
5. False. Ice forms in many shapes.
★ 6. Yes. Iron is a metal which can be turned into a liquid by heating it.
7. c) When gas is squashed into a smaller space it is called compressed.
8. b) Electrons carry an electrical charge. A flow of electrons is called electricity.
9. a) Power stations use the element uranium to make nuclear energy.
★10. Japan. The USA dropped two nuclear bombs there in 1945.
11. c) A microscope which uses lenses to magnify an object is called an optical microscope.

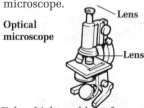

Optical microscope Lens Lens

12. False. Light and heat from stars is released by nuclear energy.
★13. Smells are gases. Smells spread because gas molecules move easily.
★14. Divers, astronauts and fire fighters carry compressed oxygen in tanks.
15. The three elements are gold, copper and oxygen.

Using materials

★ 1. Oil and fuel; iron ore and bridge; tree and book; clay and crockery; wool and sweater; cocoa and chocolate. Score a point if you got them all right.
2. c) Nylon is a man-made material.
3. a) Texas, USA is famous for crude oil.

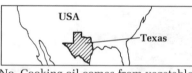

USA Texas

★ 4. No. Cooking oil comes from vegetables.
★ 5. The racing car needs to be light in weight to help it travel faster.
★ 6. Rubber comes from latex – the sap of a rubber tree. Score a point if you guessed it was a plant or a tree.

The trunk of the tree is cut. **Latex flows out.**

★ 7. The suit has to be fire-resistant to protect the driver if the car crashes, and oil and fuel catch fire.
8. No. Crude oil cannot be used in cars as fuel. It has to be refined first.
9. b) People first made alloys in the Bronze Age. Bronze is an alloy of the metals copper and tin.
10. True. More than three-quarters of all elements are metals.
11. c) This is called a blast furnace. Air is blasted, or blown, into it.
12. True. Many metals react, or change, if they come into contact with air or water. Some metals, such as sodium or potassium, may even explode. For this reason, they are stored in oil.
13. c) The purity of gold is measured in carats. A carat is the amount of pure gold mixed with other metals in an object. 24 carat gold is pure gold.
14. False.
15. a) A thin sheet of gold is called gold leaf. It can be used to cover cheaper metals.

Moving, flying and floating

1. True. Friction does not act in space, and the weak gravity between the earth and moon has very little effect on a fast-moving spaceship.
★ 2. Yes. Stone is more dense than chocolate. The material in it is packed closer together.
3. False. Steel is made from iron and carbon. Over 90% of metal produced is either iron or steel.
★ 4. Cyclists crouch low so that air flows over them smoothly, enabling them to go faster.
5. a) A tandem is a bike for two riders.

Tandem

★ 6. You feel more friction on gravel. Ice has a very smooth surface, so things slide over it, rather than grip it.
7. c) Sliding down a rope might give you a friction burn.
8. True. Most birds have hollow bones to make them lighter. This makes it easier for them to take off and fly.

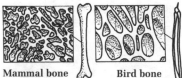

Mammal bone   **Bird bone**

9. b) The first people to fly used aircraft driven by propellers.
★10. No. Helicopters have blades. These lift the aircraft into the air directly, making a wing unnecessary.

Rotor blades

Helicopter

11. True. Gliders fly without engines. They are made with light materials, and glide in patches of warm air.
12. An empty ship would sit higher in the sea. A heavy cargo pushes the ship's hull farther down against the upthrust of the water underneath it.
★13. Cork floats. It is less dense than water.
14. c) A submarine dives by filling compartments, called ballast tanks, with water. This makes it heavier than water so it sinks. It surfaces by filling these tanks with a supply of compressed air.

Submarine on surface.

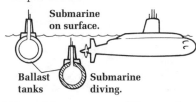

Ballast tanks   **Submarine diving.**

15. b) Isaac Newton was well known for studying mathematics.

Making things work

1. A piece of stretched elastic has potential energy, which will be released when the elastic is let go.

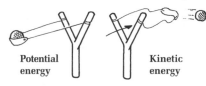

Potential energy   **Kinetic energy**

2. False. Steam has more energy than hot water, because it is hotter and its molecules are moving faster.
★ 3. You would find the following forms of energy in lightning: heat, light, electrical and kinetic. Score a point if you got two or more.
4. b) The first nuclear power station opened in 1956.
5. Yes. Sound can travel through walls.
6. True. Animal manure can be used to produce energy. When it rots it gives off a gas called methane, or biogas. Millions of people in China already use this gas as a fuel.

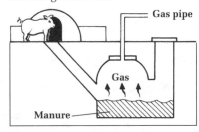

Gas pipe

Gas

Manure

7. b) Oil, coal and natural gas are called fossil fuels.
8. True. The sun evaporates water from the earth's surface. The water then condenses to form clouds and falls as rain. This cycle of water would not be possible without heat from the sun.
9. a) Uranium is a type of metal.
★10. A burning candle produces heat and light energy.
11. c) Sound cannot travel through space because there are no air particles to pass on sound waves.
12. True. Most energy produced by a light bulb is heat.
13. a) Energy in food is measured in Calories.

This cake has 300 Calories.   **This celery has 8 Calories.**

14. A fat person has more stored energy than a thin person. If you eat more food than your body uses for energy, the extra is stored in your body as fat.
★15. Yes. Even when you are asleep, your body still uses energy.

You digest food.   **Your heart beats**

You breathe.

Electricity and magnetism

1. No. Brass, like all metals, is a conductor of electricity.
★ 2. No. Some turbines are turned by running water, for example in hydroelectric power stations. The wind can also work turbines.

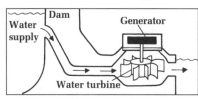

Dam   **Generator**   **Water supply**   **Water turbine**

3. False. Thunder is caused by lightning heating up the air it passes through. The air expands rapidly, creating a bang.
★ 4. Lightning always hits the highest point on the ground beneath it. This is why tall buildings have lightning rods to draw the lightning to them, rather than the building they are on.
5. a) Hair standing on end can be caused by static electricity.
6. False. There is nothing to stop lightning from striking the same place, such as a lightning rod, twice.
7. True. Your heart makes tiny electric shocks to keep it beating. These shocks can be measured by a machine called an electrocardiograph.

Electrocardiographs record your heartbeat in a pattern like this.

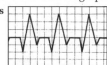

8. a) Rubber boots. Rubber is a very good insulator. If you were to touch a live electric wire while wearing rubber boots, the rubber would prevent the electricity from flowing through you and reaching the ground.
★ 9. It is unsafe because water could seep into the appliance and conduct electricity to your body. This could give you a dangerous electric shock.
★10. No. Wood is not a magnetic material.
★11. Yes. The earth has a metal core, which has a magnetic field. This makes the magnetic material in a compass needle point north.

The magnetic field of earth.   **North**

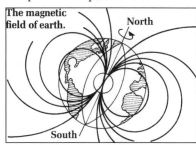

South

12. No. Glue picks up material because it is sticky. It has no magnetic quality.
13. c) Watts are units of electrical power.
14. d) A washing machine uses an electric motor.
★15. c) The electric motor was invented in England, in 1821, by Michael Faraday.

Sound and music

1. A clap of thunder is louder than a handclap, so it has more energy.
2. c) The loudness of sound is measured in decibels (or dB).
★ 3. Yes. Sound travels around corners. Sound waves spread out as they go through gaps or around obstacles.
4. False. The bones in the middle ear are called the hammer, anvil and stirrup.

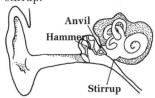

Anvil
Hammer
Stirrup

5. a) Balance. Inside your ear are three semi-circular tubes. These contain liquid which flows against tiny hair cells when you move. These cells send signals to your brain telling you which way you have moved.
6. True. Fish pick up sound vibrations with a tube-like organ called the lateral line, which runs along their bodies.

Lateral line

★ 7. Yes. Children can hear higher frequencies than adults.
★ 8. You would hear an echo better on a calm day. On a windy day, returning sound waves would be scattered.
9. False. However, some sounds can travel a very long way, especially in water. Underwater loudspeakers can make sounds in the Antarctic, that scientists can detect in the Arctic.

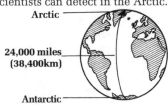

Arctic

24,000 miles
(38,400km)

Antarctic

10. b) Locating objects by listening to high frequency echoes is called sonar. It stands for SOund, NAvigation and Ranging.
11. False.
12. True. The sound humpback whales make has specific notes and patterns which they repeat, like a bird's song.
13. a) Drums, cymbals and xylophones are all percussion instruments. This type of instrument is struck to make sounds.
14. Angor, batu, napio and tirgua can be unscrambled to make these instruments.

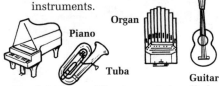

Organ
Piano
Tuba
Guitar

15. c) A place without any air is called a vacuum.

Light and color

1. c) Red and yellow make orange.
2. b) Another name for the colors of the rainbow is a spectrum.
3. No. Light travels in straight lines. Light can only go around a corner if it is reflected off a surface.

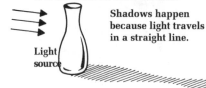

Shadows happen because light travels in a straight line.

Light source

4. False. Most animals have color vision, but some, such as dogs, can only see in black-and-white.
5. True. Fireflies and some sea animals make light with chemicals produced inside them. They make light to attract a mate or to lure food.

Firefly

Light-producing chemicals are made here.

6. Snow reflects all the colors in white light equally well.
7. c) The sea is blue because it reflects the sky, which is also blue.
★ 8. Yes. Light can travel through space. If it could not, we would have no sunlight on earth.
9. True. Ancient Egyptians made mirrors from polished bronze metal.

Egyptian mirror

★ 10. Yes. Polished wood is fairly smooth. Some light is reflected evenly off this smooth surface, so you see a reflection.
11. False. The eye is filled with fluid. This helps bend light towards the retina.

This part of the eye is filled with a watery fluid.

This part of the eye is filled with a jelly-like fluid.

Eye

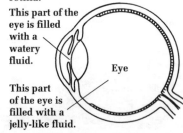

★ 12. You need to blink in order to clean the surface of the eye.
13. a) This part of the eye is called the cornea. Along with the lens and eye fluids, it focuses light on the retina.
14. b) Cats and c) owls can see well in the dark. They hunt at night because there is less competition for food.
★ 15. Lightning travels faster than thunder. Thunder and lightning happen at the same time, but lightning reaches you first because light travels faster than sound.

Living things

1. c) Plants do not think. However, some can react very quickly. For example, when you touch a mimosa plant, its leaves collapse. This may shake off insects that are trying to eat it.
2. False. An erupting volcano is no more alive than the wind and the rain.
3. b) This animal is an orangutan.
★ 4. A stick insect is an animal. It looks like a twig.

Stick insect

5. True. There are several plants, such as the venus flytrap, which catch and eat insects and other small animals.

The venus flytrap

★ 6. These plants are called sunflowers.
7. False. Plants grow towards sunlight to absorb as much energy as possible.
8. c) The pancreas is not a bone. It is a group of cells, called a gland, which produces digestive juices.

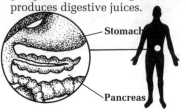

Stomach
Pancreas

★ 9. No. Your brain is not a muscle. It is an organ. An organ is a specific part of the body, such as the heart or the liver, which does a particular job.
10. a) In the womb, a baby is attached to the mother by the umbilical cord, which suppplies it with food and oxygen.

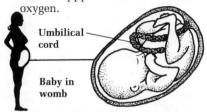

Umbilical cord

Baby in womb

11. An egg cell is much bigger than a sperm cell.
12. c) Protein, found in meat, cheese and fish, is essential for growth.
13. True. When you get up in the morning, you are at full height. During the day, gravity presses down on you and closes the tiny gaps between your joints. By the evening you are a little shorter.
14. True. There are 206 bones in your body, including 32 in each arm and 31 in each leg.
15. a) Your nails never stop growing while you are alive.

Evolution

1. False. Scientists think that domestic cats have evolved from wild cats, possibly from Africa.
★ 2. No. You should not eat horse chestnut seeds, but you can bake and eat the seeds of sweet chestnut trees.

Horse chestnut   Sweet chestnut

3. Yes. Animals with short life spans and many offspring evolve quicker, because any change in their appearance or the way they act will be passed on to their own offspring much quicker.
★ 4. Moths usually come out at night.
5. False.
6. b) The armadillo is not extinct. Armadillos are found in North and South America, and have thick bony plates around their bodies to protect them from predators.

Armadillo

★ 7. Present day tigers have stripes to help them blend in with the light and shade of the forests they inhabit.

Modern tiger   Saber-toothed tiger

8. No. Wisdom teeth are found in all sorts of people.
9. a) Eyebrows help to keep sweat from the brow out of the eyes.
10. b) Most scientists think the first humans lived in Africa.
11. a) Pedigree dogs. A dog must have ancestors of the same breed for three generations (back to its great grandparents), to be a pedigree dog.
12. c) The husky is most like a wolf.

Husky   Wolf

13. No. Lions are the product of natural selection in the wild. They are too fierce and dangerous to be of any practical use to humans.
★ 14. The mule is a cross between a donkey and a horse. Mules are strong animals, but they cannot usually have their own offspring.
15. c) Genetic engineering is a branch of biotechnology.

The balance of nature

1. False. The study of living things in the environment is called ecology.
2. b) Protecting the environment is called conservation.
★ 3. Hawks hunt by day, when they make the best use of their sharp eyesight.

Sparrowhawks hide in trees and ambush their prey.

4. The thrush has more choice of food than the owl. It is an omnivore, eating both plants and animals.
5. In this particular food web, rabbits need to watch out for foxes.
6. False. Many large animals, such as elephants and horses, are herbivores.
★ 7. Humans are omnivores.
8. There would be more caterpillars than hawks in a forest food web. For a food web to feed all its animals, there have to be more animals at the lower end to provide food for those at the top.
9. b) The boring beetle is a real beetle.

Boring beetles burrow into trees.

10. a) Sites where waste is buried are called landfills.
★ 11. Chernobyl power station caused much pollution when it exploded in 1986. Large parts of the former Soviet Union and Northern Europe were affected.

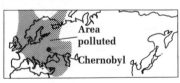

Area polluted

Chernobyl

★ 12. Yes. Almost half the iron used to make steel is recycled. Recycling iron is cheaper, and uses less energy than making new iron from iron ore.
13. c) Compost heaps take around six months to rot.
14. b) Materials that rot are called biodegradable, which means they can be broken down by bacteria. Materials made from living things are able to rot, but metals, glass and most plastics do not rot.

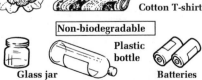

Biodegradable

Cauliflower   Newspaper

Cotton T-shirt

Non-biodegradable

Plastic bottle

Glass jar   Batteries

15. True. In 1990, Americans threw away nearly 4lbs (2kg) of waste a day.

Science and technology

1. b) CDs are coated with a protective layer of transparent plastic.
★ 2. No. Written information and pictures can also be stored on CD.
3. c) The picture has been magnified around 8,000 times.
4. False. CDs are very hard-wearing. It is unlikely that they will wear out. Unlike records and tapes which rub against another hard surface, the CD surface is only touched by light.
5. True. Lasers are used to read bar codes. The reflections of the laser beam form a digital code, which registers the price of goods.

Bar code

White reflects light.   Black does not reflect light.

9   7 0 7 4 6   1 1 2 7 4

★ 6. Yes. Laser light travels in a straight line and is used to measure distances.

Lasers have measured the distance between the earth and the moon.

Moon   Earth

238,000 miles
384,000km

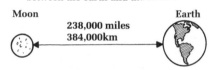

7. True. Some lasers are brighter than the Sun. Scientists are trying to find a way to use bright lasers to generate nuclear power.
8. c) All new cars in the USA are fitted with catalytic converters.
★ 9. Yes. Exhaust fumes are acidic. They dissolve in moisture in the air, which then falls as acid rain.

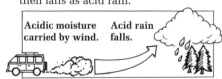

Acidic moisture carried by wind.   Acid rain falls.

10. False. Breathing carbon monoxide will not make your hair go white, but it is poisonous. If you breathe a great deal of it, it can kill you.
11. a) Energy efficient light bulbs last 8 times longer than ordinary bulbs.
12. False. Energy efficient light bulbs work as long as there is an electricity supply.
13. Camcorder stands for CAMera and reCORDER.
14. True. There are about 400,000 pixels on a CCD.
★ 15. A palmcorder is a very small, modern camcorder, named because it can be held in one hand. The lightest ones weigh around 1lb 12oz (800g).

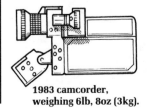

1993 palmcorder.

1983 camcorder, weighing 6lb, 8oz (3kg).

Science Megaquiz answers

There are 100 possible points in the whole Science Megaquiz. Score a point for each correct answer. If you score over 50 you have done well. Over 75 is excellent. You can find out more about some of the answers on the page listed after it.

Misfits

1. The pinna is not part of the eye.
2. Original is not a type of energy.
3. Density is not a force.
4. Brown is not a color of the rainbow.
5. A lightbulb does not make electricity.
6. Magnetism is not a feature of all living things.
7. The mammoth is extinct.
8. A siphon is not part of an atom.
9. A baby is not a cell.
10. Flutes are not percussion instruments.

Inventions and discoveries

1. Spectacles (c).
2. Mercury thermometer (f).
3. Powered flight (h).
4. Nuclear energy (i).
5. Evolution (g).
6. Camcorder (j).
7. Gravity (e).
8. Smelting iron (b).
9. Wheel (a).
10. The earth goes around the sun (d).

Talking science

1. Sunset (page 48).
2. Compost (page 55).
3. Elements (page 36).
4. Field (page 45).
5. Prism (page 48).
6. Food (page 54).
7. Gravity (page 40).
8. Galaxy (page 34).
9. Pollution (page 57).
10. Insulator (page 44).

Materials

1. c) metal (page 44).
2. Hydrocarbons/nitrogen/carbon monoxide (page 57).
3. c) trees (pages 38-39).
4. A compound (page 36).
5. Animal skin (page 38).
6. Gold (page 39).
7. Hydrogen (page 34).
8. b) water (page 51).
9. Copper (page 44).
10. c) clay (pages 42-43).

Close-ups

1. Owl (page 54).
2. Radio telescope (page 34).
3. Suspension springs (page 39).
4. Peppered moth (page 52).
5. Camcorder (page 57).
6. Cell (page 50).
7. Atoms (page 36).
8. Cow (page 42).
9. Eye (page 49).
10. Compact disc (page 56).

Animals and plants

1. (d) berries.
2. (c) blue whale.
3. (a) white cat.
4. (g) horse chestnut seed.
5. (b) bat.
6. (e) saber-toothed tiger.
7. (i) old English sheepdog.
8. (j) orangutan.
9. (h) puffin.
10. (f) rabbit.

True or false?

1. True (page 35).
2. False.
3. False.
4. True (page 48).
5. True (page 51).
6. False.
7. True (page 37).
8. False.
9. False.
10. True (page 46).

Silhouettes

1. Hawk (page 54).
2. Spring (page 42).
3. Ship (page 41).
4. Coccyx (page 53).
5. Balloon (page 36).
6. Wisdom tooth (page 53).
7. Guitar (page 47).
8. Nerve cell (page 51).
9. Atom (page 37).
10. Caterpillar (page 50).

Body bits

1. Blood (page 43).
2. Appendix (page 53).
3. Pituitary gland (page 51).
4. Optic nerve (page 49).
5. Skin.
6. Muscles (page 51).
7. Skeleton (page 51).
8. Iris (page 49).
9. Coccyx (page 53).
10. Pinna (page 46).

What do you know?

1. Photosynthesis (page 50).
2. Static electricity (page 44).
3. Compact disc (page 56).
4. Yes, with an electron microscope.
5. a) 15 thousand (page 34).
6. Ores (page 38).
7. Magnetism (page 45).
8. b) silk (page 38).
9. Laser light (page 56).
10. Plants (page 54).

Scientists and inventors

Below are some scientists and inventors who contributed to ideas and inventions in Part Two of this book.

Carothers, Wallace 1896-1937
American chemist who discovered nylon (pages 38-39), which was the first man-made fiber to be widely used.

Dalton, John 1766-1844
English self-taught chemist who carried out important research into the existence of atoms (pages 36-37).

Darwin, Charles 1809-1882
English naturalist, who proposed the natural selection theory of evolution (pages 52-53).

Dunlop, John 1840-1921
Scottish veterinary surgeon who invented the first air-filled tire, called the pneumatic tire (page 38).

Einstein, Albert 1879-1955
German physicist who made many important discoveries concerning nuclear energy (page 37) and light (pages 48-49).

Faraday, Michael 1791-1867
English scientist who invented the electric motor (page 45).

Franklin, Benjamin 1706-1790
American scientist and politician who showed that lightning is a form of electricity. He also invented the lightning rod (page 44).

Galilei, Galileo, 1564-1642
Italian physicist who was one of the first people to use a telescope to study the solar system (page 34).

Goddard, Robert 1882-1945
American physicist who was a leading figure in the development of the space rocket (page 35). He launched the first liquid-fuelled rocket in 1926.

Lemaitre, Georges 1894-1966
Belgian astronomer who first suggested the Big Bang theory (page 34).

Mendel, Gregor 1822-1884
Austrian monk who discovered that living things pass on characteristics to their offspring (page 52).

Newton, Isaac 1642-1727
English mathematician and physicist who proved light was a mixture of colors (pages 48-49) and proposed theories on gravity and motion (pages 40-41).

Watt, James 1736-1819
Scottish engineer who developed the steam engine. The watt, a unit of electrical power (page 45), is named after him.

The publishers would like to thank the following for the use of their photographs and reference material in this section of the book: NRSC LTD/Science Photo Library (page 35, left); Dr. Mitsuo Ohtsuki/Science Photo Library (page 37, bottom right); Canon (UK) Ltd (page 57, top).